D1625311

More
Lightning
Less
Thunder

"Thunder is good,
thunder is impressive,
but it is the lightning
that does the work."

- Mark Twain

How to
Energize Innovation Teams

BOB ECKERT & JONATHAN VEHAR

About This Book:

More Lightning, Less Thunder: How to Energize Innovation Teams is a light-hearted look at the serious topic of working with others to create innovation.

One person *can* make a difference. But in organizations, we have to work in groups and teams. And despite our best intentions, abilities, and skills, all those other people keep getting in the way! Yet...

This book gives our best answer to the question with which we've been alligator-wrestling for a long time: "Besides process, tools, and techniques for thinking creatively and working together in teams, what else do you need in order to integrate these things so you can work better with other people?"

This book is designed to alter the fundamental behaviors and specific attitudes necessary for *individuals* to function in a team environment. It's designed so that when you're working with teams, you can work together more effectively and innovatively, with a dramatic reduction in non-productive interaction. Day after day in our work with large corporations and small not-for-profits we see that what individuals need are specific behaviors that are critical for creativity, innovation, and teamwork to flourish within teams.

The information in this book has been delivered in workshops for a wide range of organizations to create innovation teams, from Fortune 500 to government systems, to human service organizations, to educational institutions. Large and small, they all share one variable: they are created and run by people. Read on and find out how to be a human being working with other humans to achieve success!

Need more reasons to read? Here are the benefits that can be derived from reading this book:

Improved communication with the people in your life and work

More effective leadership and followership for better use of authority

Strategies for working together effectively with difficult people

Increased tolerance for the strengths and shortcomings of self and others

Understanding of the importance of risk-taking in difficult climates

Understanding of a model for successful innovative teams

Increased trust among group members

A new attitude about your ability to innovate on teams

Enjoying working with others, even when they're not enjoyable

By the way, this book is not about THEM: the other members of the team, or the people who get in the way of innovation (although one of the possible titles of this book was, *Those Morons!*).

This book is about YOU.

Gandhi said, "you must be the change that you wish to see in the world." This book takes that philosophy to heart and launches on an exploration of what you – heck, all of us – can do in order to create innovation with a team. Want to know more about this book? Start reading it. It's self-explanatory.

More
Lightning
Less
Thunder

Bob Eckert & Jonathan Vehar

More
Lightning
Less
Thunder

How to
Energize Innovation Teams

Bob Eckert & Jonathan Vehar

Additional books may be purchased by writing to:

New & Improved®, 9306 State Route 30, Paul Smiths, NY, 12970.

Or: info@newandimproved.com

Edition 3.0.1

Editing, and extreme patience by Monica Mead

Additional editing and ultra-extreme patience by Susan Rossetti

Illustrations © 2001 by Eric James Spencer

Layout and typesetting by Catherine Tulip and Mark Roser

Cover design by Kim Erwin

More Lightning Less Thunder

How to Energize Innovation Teams

New & Improved®

LAKE PLACID, NY   EVANSTON, IL

This book is dedicated to our guiding lights, who also serve as our anchors. These inspirations go by the names of Sheila, Hannah, Luke, and Susan.

"That which you vividly imagine, sincerely believe, ardently desire, and enthusiastically act upon, will inevitably come to pass."

-- William R. Lucas

"There is more in us than we know. If we can be made to see it, perhaps, for the rest of our lives we will be unwilling to settle for less."

- Kurt Hahn, Founder, Outward Bound

Acknowledgments

This book has been stewing about in our brains and word processors for a number of years now, and with the help of a great Innovation Team of our own, it has come to pass. We would like to thank the following people for helping us think better, clearer, and more innovatively via their collaboration, debate, inspiration, and/or conversation while sipping grandé decaf low-fat no-foam café au laits (previously known simply as "coffee"):

Blair Miller	Russ Schoen
Roger Firestien	Bill Shephard
Debbie Allen	Sarah Thurber
Jon Pearson	Suzanne Chamberlain
Mary Bartlett	Dennis Carter
David Hughes	Margaret King
Gloria Rapport	Jamie O'Boyle
Doug Reid	Jerry Hirschberg
Gerard Puccio	David Gonzalez
Sylvain Matte	Gordon MacKenzie
Mark Roser	

And especially Sid Parnes and Alex Osborn, who started this all for us.

Needless to say, this book would not be nearly as interesting, readable, or fun to look at without our friends and colleagues Monica Mead, Cathy Tulip, Rose Masterpol, Eric Spencer, Jon Pearson, Rick Schin, as well as Liz and Kieran Boesen.

And we are eternally indebted to those who put up with us on a regular basis, inspiring us to be better than we think we can be, even when we don't want to be: Susan Rossetti, Robert and Persis Vehar, Gabrielle Vehar, Julie and Bob Eckert, Sr., Sheila Delarm, Hannah Eckert, and Luke Eckert. They energize our work, lives and hearts.

Table of Contents

"If you want to feel secure, do what you already know how to do.

But if you want to grow, go to the cutting edge of your competence, which means a temporary loss of security.

So whenever you don't quite know what you are doing...

know that you are growing."

Preface

"Thunder is good, thunder is impressive, but it is the lightning that does the work."

-- Mark Twain

Definition: Innovation Team -

"a number of persons deliberately working together at high levels of productivity to achieve innovative results and success."

(SOURCE: The New & Improved Post-Collegiate Dictionary)

So what's this book all about?

At a distance, it would seem to be about building innovation in teams. And in fact, it is. We want to explore just how human beings might work together more effectively to create great things, do great works, and build a healthier, more sustainable world.

Because people are *predictable* and because we've been in the business of working with people for most of our adult lives, we've learned some things that our clients have found to be valuable in improving both innovation skills and team functionality.

Because people are also *unpredictable* and because we've only been working with people for a relatively short time (given how long people have been on the earth), it is difficult to say just exactly which of our thoughts will be of value to you. Since you really are the person responsible for your learning, we encourage you to read this with an open, inquisitive mind. At one point, we considered naming the book, *Those Jerks!*, but we realized that that points the finger at others. In fact, the only person you can change is you. Darn. Make this book about you, and we guarantee you'll get value from it

Up close, this book is about the fundamental rules of the human experience. Learn the rules, play the game well, and in general your life will work pretty well for you. Be ignorant of the rules (or know but ignore them) and you're leaving your experience of life to chance. We don't know about you, but based upon our lifetime lottery winnings, we don't think turning our life over to "luck" would be a very smart move.

A final warning. We're writing about serious stuff. But we've lived long enough to not take ourselves so seriously, and you'll see it reflected in our writing. We tend to be a bit irreverent. If we're serious about anything at all, it's our irreverence.

It's a scientific fact that sometimes life stinks. And no stupid book is going to change that fact. The best we can hope to do is decrease the time we spend in the unpleasant times and increase the frequency and duration of the good times. If you find someone who says they can fix it for good, run like you stole something. Better yet, lock-'em up. We have enough megalomania in the world already.

So...

What do you want this book to teach
you about you?

Introduction

"Problems become opportunities when the right people come together."

- Robert Redford

One person can make a difference. Think China. Student protests. Remember the picture of the protestor in the short-sleeve shirt with his briefcase standing in the path of a tank in Tiananmen Square in order to protect the protesters? Unforgettable. He made a difference.

In organizations, however, we have to work in groups and teams. Some of whom get in the way of making a difference. The results of which we wish were forgettable! So now what!?

Business consulting guru Tom Peters, in his last bestseller, "The Circle of Innovation," (which we highly recommend) begins chapter six with these words,

"Jog down to your local bookstore. Check the business shelves. Bet #1: Ten or more books on creating the self-managing factory work team. Bet #2: No books on creating the GREAT Purchasing Department…the GREAT Finance Department…the GREAT Engineering Department. Why? Beats me."

Peters then goes on to list 28 ways to create a GREAT department, including things to think about, get trained in, and to focus on. That's a great start!

One person CAN make a difference

Yet in our vast (and half-vast) years of working with a wide variety of clients to help them achieve great innovative results with their departments, we've discovered that there are also fundamental attitudes and beliefs necessary for true teamwork. And while it's important…even critical…to "T-h-i-n-k client!" and Peters' other 27 suggested steps. It's just as important to shift and integrate the attitudes necessary to do just that.

So once again we ask, "Now what!?" How do we create a team that is more than the sum of its parts?

This book gives you our best answer to this question: "In addition to tools and techniques for thinking creatively and working together in teams (which are important!), what else do you need to integrate this stuff and make it work?"

There are lots of books on process, tools, and techniques for innovation, problem solving, creativity, leadership, and teamwork, many of which we like and use. But that's just the start. We've discovered that what's needed are attitudes and behaviors that are critical for creativity, innovation, and teamwork to flourish. "What behaviors?" you ask.

Glad you asked…

Congratulations!

You've just been appointed to the team to carry out your dream project. The one project that means more to you than anything in the world. The passion you have for seeing the project through to its successful conclusion is unparalleled. Nothing is more critical to you. You couldn't be happier to be a part of the team.

And you're excited about working with a team rather than by yourself, because you know the team will generate more creative and innovative solutions, thus increasing the likelihood of success. There are multiple talents to draw from, and multiple energies to get the job done.

So just what kind of team are you hoping to work with? A bunch of arrogant self-righteous types who won't try anything new? People who don't let anybody know what is going on and never listen to you when you try to talk to them? How about people who insist on always being the winner even if that means giving up on making things work as well as they can? Better yet, how would you like to work with team members who won't start anything important, and worse yet, won't finish it?

What, are you crazy?

Why would you willingly or knowingly subject yourself to working with such a bunch of jerks? You wouldn't. Not willingly or knowingly…at least not if you have a choice.

Unfortunately we (and by "we" we mean you and Bob and Jonathan…all of us) do this ALL THE TIME!! What's wrong with us? Why would we sabotage our projects and our functionality by working with people who just don't get it!? There are lots of reasons. Usually it's because we don't have a choice. We're either assigned to the team at work, or we're part of a group of volunteers, or that's just the nature of the group we find ourselves on.

Rats! There just aren't enough perfect people to go around. And truthfully, there are times that even our contribution to smooth team functioning leaves a little to be desired. Imagine that!

So it's true, we don't always have a choice of the people with WHOM we work, but we do have a choice of HOW we work. Unfortunately, you don't have a choice of how the other people behave. (Unless you can convince them to integrate what's in this book).

And that's the point. No, not to convince them to read this book (not that we'll argue with that), but rather, to help build groups of individuals who hold themselves to a higher standard. A standard that enables them to work together to create tremendous results that enable innovation. Consider this book to have the following **purpose**:

TO HELP YOU ESTABLISH BEHAVIORS THAT LEAD TO PEOPLE WORKING TOGETHER PRODUCTIVELY TO CREATE INNOVATIVE AND SUCCESSFUL RESULTS.

* * *

What we know about groups and teams and innovation could fill a book (hmmm). And not coincidently, much of it is in here. We've been working with a huge range of groups to make creativity happen for years in a wide variety of organizations. From Fortune 10's to family businesses to not-for-profit organizations to human service to government to healthcare to churches to our families.

We find that they really only have one thing in common. Mind you it's one pretty important thing! All organizations depend on people. And fortunately, as much as all people are different (like organizations), they're also the same in many respects. Once they let go of the notion that they must play by the usual (dysfunctional) group rules-norms-practices, amazing things happen. Namely, people do great things, move (figurative)

mountains, achieve innovative results, succeed like never before, and enjoy what they're doing.

Sound like something worth pursuing? We thought so too. So here then are our seven guidelines for working together. We pursue each in great depth in the body of the book complete with suggestions on how to implement these practices. These are our 7 rules for creating an Innovation Team:

1 - Surrender to Your Humanity

Let's face it. Nobody's perfect. Yet amazingly, we expect that of ourselves and everyone else we deal with. And 1) we're unwilling to settle for anything less. Which is fine, but it doesn't equate to reality. It doesn't equate to a world where everybody is a human being, and 2) human beings will, and do, make mistakes. And 1 + 2 creates an unworkable group attitude of resentment. Not a good thing.

THE MOTTO: *We're all human, and we all make mistakes. That's just the way it is. Get used to it.*

2 - Understand Responsibility

We really have only one responsibility. And that's to choose how we react to everything that happens around us. We can't control external events, just how we choose to interpret what they mean for us.

THE MOTTO: *I have the ability to react to anything however I want. So I'm going to make the reaction a good one!*

3 - Consciously Listen / Clearly Speak

Communication is hard. (We've been doing it all our lives, the two of us have been professionally studying it and teaching it for over 15 years each, and we still blow it. Not occasionally, but regularly.) Don't believe us? Ask your boss, our wives, all of our clients. They'll tell you. So how do you manage to get it right? Focus on a) listening and only listening. Forget about responding. Forget about trying to solve it. Just listen. Then focus on b) clearly expressing yourself in a way that makes it possible for you to be heard. That means communicating clearly, crisply, and then making sure you were understood.

THE MOTTO: *We need to listen to understand, then speak so we can be understood. Then we need to make sure everybody got it right!*

4 - Cultivate Risk-Taking

Playing it safe doesn't accomplish innovation or energize creativity. It breeds the status quo. Not quite what we're going for here, is it? More important than tolerating misteaks (see "Surrender to Your Humanity" above) is actually encouraging them and, in fact, striving for them! Setting a quota of mistakes (we use a quota of 30 mistakes per hour) that you not only CAN make but in fact WILL make will get you closer to new discoveries, new ways of doing things, reinventing how to be, and learning anew. The motto "we learn more from our mistakes than our successes" has been replaced with, "we learn ONLY when we're willing to make mistakes." Period. Exclamation point.

THE MOTTO: *I learn only when I'm willing to make mistakes. Today I want to learn a lot, so I'm expecting lots of mistakes!*

5 - Expect Win/Win

You'll notice that these don't get any easier. Here it's simple. Really, really difficult to practice, but it's a simple concept. Stop trying to win at all costs. Unless you're trying for EVERYONE to win. So that no one loses. Not you, not the other person, not the buyer, not the seller, not even your enemies. Make it about trying to set up an environment where people are in it for everyone to be successful. So that everybody wins and so that today's loser doesn't become tomorrow's mean-and-vindictive-out-to-get-you-jerk-from-hell-on-wheels. Hey, you never know what situation you'll be in tomorrow and with whom you'll have to work.

THE MOTTO: *In order for us to be successful, (unlike the lottery) everybody has to be the big winner.*

6 - Strive for Continuous Improvement

The proverbial ball never stops moving. Your competitor's quality level never stays the same. Your need to serve your clients never diminishes. The budget almost never goes up, and resources usually shrink. The world is different now than it was 10 minutes ago. People around you are changing, your family is evolving, your kids are growing. Need more reasons to keep trying to make things better? How about one more: The environment around you is changing. To survive, you MUST adapt to those changes. The only way to do that is to increase your range of responses, to be adaptable, flexible, and constantly evolving.

THE MOTTO: *Nothing, including me, is ever perfect. Everything, including me, can always be better. So I'm going to keep working on me.*

7 - Start…Finish…Start Again

So, does that make sense? Think you've got it? Happy with where you are? Great. You're done! And if you believe that…Hah! 'Fraid not you arrogant fool! The world doesn't stay the same, and you're never done growing, learning, and moving forward. There are two kinds of people in the world: people who are growing up, and people who are trapped in a rut. There are no "grown ups," just "stuck people" or "grow*ing*-ups." So celebrate when you've accomplished your goals (that's important!), and then set new ones and begin again. The world keeps advancing (see number 6 above) and you need to as well. Or be left in the dust.

THE MOTTO: *I'm never perfect. When I remain vigilant for my arrogance, I find my next opportunity for improvement.*

* * *

These basic tenets are what working together for innovation is all about. They're just that simple and basic. And just so incredibly difficult that we all have to spend our entire lives working on them. If these things were easy, we wouldn't find ourselves so frustrated at other people and beating our (figurative) heads against the (metaphorical) wall when trying to work in groups. These things take work, but it's worth it.

Cleverly concealed in these guidelines are all the things that we know are important. All the "motherhoods" that we all aspire to, like trust, teamwork, communication, openness, creativity, patience, loyalty, yada, yada, yada. These are the things that everybody talks about, and puts in their mission, vision, and values statements that are engraved in a brass plaque in the lobby. And these are the things that we have so much difficulty putting into action and sustaining in our lives.

Why? Because they're hard, and more to the point because these are lessons that we never really fully learn. Because we're never done! The second we all think we understand it, and really know how to do it, we're stuck in the trap. And that means we don't know how to do it. Darn! Curses! Foiled again!

This doesn't mean it's hopeless, just that we SHOULD be continually deepening our understanding of how to make these things happen for ourselves.

So, want to figure out how to do that? Read on!

What do you hope to get out of
this book that is -- to you --
important enough to make it worth
your time to read?

1

Surrender to
your Humanity

"You grow up the day you have your first real laugh -- at yourself."

-- Ethel Barrymore

You are a human being. Nothing more, nothing less. Ergo, you can never be perfect even though you can do some pretty amazing things. So stop wasting time and energy being ashamed when you mess up. Quit pretending you know what you are doing and what you are talking about when you're not really sure.

We waste way too much energy in the cover-up. It's a conspiracy: We all have to pretend that we're a little more together than we really are and because of that, we're all really afraid of making mistakes and being found out. So we've developed all of these duck and cover strategies that get right smack in the way of innovation.

We deny that it's our mistake…and blame the other person for not understanding.

We project the problem on to someone else…our spouse, the politicians, gravity.

Even now in your mind you're thinking about how other people do this, and not seeing as easily how this is about you.

We whine about how haarrddd it is.

So humble up. You're a screw up and you know it. Just like everyone else in the world. When we get this, when we really surrender to our humanity, we stop being so judgmental of other people when we see them mess up. It's the end of "holier than thou" as we know it. A shift in attitude that makes us a lot more fun to be around. People become drawn to us. They're willing to try out new thinking and different skills when we're around. They're growing and learning… we're growing and learning…because of our humility, we're more open to their ideas. And this, my friend, is the seedbed of Innovation Teams.

There is no such thing as a grown-up. Just growing-ups and stuck people. That's it. Your choice.

> **We waste too much energy in the cover-up**

Overriding Your Gator Brain

Human beings are wonderful creatures capable of great, loving altruistic acts. We're also capable of some pretty terrible things as well.

It's helpful for this discussion to look at the brain as three different brains working together. Our cortex which is our thinking brain, our limbic system which is our feeling brain, and our brain stem which is our survival brain. We can literally lose parts of our cortex and limbic area and still function. We cannot lose parts of our brain stem and do the same.

Our most basic survival behaviors are run by our brainstem. We call this part of our brain the gator brain because it is similar to the brain of the alligator in its entirety. Now, an alligator's existence is a pretty basic thing. Find food, protect your territory, reproduce. (Our wives say this is the autobiographical section of the book).

Animals, which have evolved in a particular environmental niche, regard any change in that niche as a threat to their very existence. Less complex animals like the reptiles have three choices in terms of how they might deal with that "newness:" Kill it. Eat it. Run from it.

We have a reptile living in our brainstem.

Our natural reaction when we see newness is the same as a gator's to an extent. Fortunately, we have a cortex, which has the ability to override the primitive instincts of the brain stem. We can treat newness with curiosity. We can defer judgment and look for the possibilities that exist in new ideas. We can be smarter than the gators if we choose to be. Innovation Teams are smarter than gators most of the time (notice we did not say "all of the time"). Individuals on Innovation Teams have re-habituated themselves so that their first response to newness is to understand it fully before they assess its potential value. It's their pathway out of the swamp. Dry feet are a wonderful thing.

Willingness to Learn: Growing-ups vs. Stuck People

How old are you when you're finally a grown up? When we were eight, we thought you had to be in your teens. When we were in our teens, we thought it was 20. Then 25. Then 30. Then 40 seemed like it might be a magical year.

We gave up trying to figure it out when we realized that there is no such thing as a grown-up. Not even at 70? Nope, we're never done. A little burnt-out every once in a while, but never done.

After all, how old are you when you know it all? Sixteen or seventeen, right? And then you realize that you really don't know it all, and your parents really do know something after all. And that there's a lot of knowledge and wisdom in the world to grab hold of.

We're never finished growing. But sometimes we stop being willing to learn. We get our heads stuck so firmly up our attitude that we think we have to know everything in order to do our job. That in order to create new ideas we must have complete knowledge. But it's impossible. And as soon as we realize that we're never going to know everything, we stop needing to pretend that we do. Then we get unstuck. We get open. We get curious. We create.

Have you read this before in this book? We hope so. Will you read it again? You betcha. Why? This is one of the most difficult lessons to internalize that we know of. Just last week Jonathan had to learn it again! Bob too! And while that's true as we write this, we also know that two weeks prior to your reading it, it will also be true. Would that it weren't so, but…

When we do our Innovation Team trainings, we first talk about this issue intellectually, then give the group challenges to overcome which are easy if they are successfully overriding their gator brains. Invariably the groups fail at these simple tasks that we've selected for their uncanny ability to hook humans' more primitive behaviors. It takes a whole series of these challenges before the individuals in the group finally get enough humility to begin being aggressively vigilant for their own personal gator brain behaviors. And we find that that vigilance must be constantly re-energized. Even as you read this, it's difficult not to fall into the trap of thinking that you'd get that lesson quicker than other people, and that you'd solve the problems we gave you in a more "evolved" way. Wanna bet? You'll lose. Are we making you mad yet? Good. Prove us wrong. Be vigilant for the part of you that is sure you're more together than the next person. Energize your humility. Create a space for growth in your life.

We'll say it again. There are no such thing as grown-ups just growing-ups and stuck people.

Which one would you rather be?

The Humble Group

We've been working to build high function groups for a long time now, and over time, we've changed our minds about the best way to do that. Initially we used "high adventure" challenges, which the group initially perceived to be just about impossible to overcome. In spite of their perceptions, we knew that if they called fully on the resources of the group's members, they would succeed. In those days, we earned our chops as trainers by choosing challenges for the group, which would have them a hair away from disaster and still succeed.

The result was something we called "group esteem"-a high energy warm fuzzy feeling about being on the team. The fact is that they were a little arrogant and full of themselves. A recipe for disaster back at the work site. "We don't have to *work* to be a team, we *are* a team! We climbed Mt. Muckettymuckmuck!

These days, we're strong advocates of what we are calling "group humility." From a training perspective, we get there now by giving the group challenges that are perceived as easily overcome, but are chosen for their uncanny ability to cause the group to behave in unproductive patterns that they know *intellectually* are unproductive…yet they *behave* unproductively anyway. The *choice* to behave as a high function innovation team is always there, and the group agrees intellectually that it would be the better way to go, but they are unable to step up to the challenge of doing so.

A very humbling insight.

And one that creates *vigilance* for unproductive behaviors instead of arrogance.

The dynamic of living and working as a member of an innovation team is that it goes against the grain of our protective gator brain behaviors. And that gator is a slimy creature and will slither out and rear its ugly head any chance it gets. We need to remain constantly vigilant for unproductive thinking and behavior patterns if we want to be on an innovation team. Humility helps.

The Value of Playfulness and Humor in the Workplace

We take ourselves so seriously. Too seriously. We believe that in order to do a good job, to do it right, we must be serious. Not true! We may be doing serious work...flying planes, making cars, taking care of patients, managing a company, teaching students, keeping the books...but that doesn't mean that we need to be serious all the time or to take ourselves seriously as we do our jobs. It's possible to do serious work without being serious.

In fact it's actually counterproductive to do it any other way. Research on environments that foster innovation show that playfulness and humor are critically supportive elements. We can be serious about what we're doing without taking ourselves seriously, and we must.

So laugh a little. See the humor in your mistakes. Play (harmless and loving) practical jokes on one another. Let go of the need to look like you're completely in charge of your emotions and above all the frivolity. Above the *ability* to laugh. Above the *need* to laugh.

In the words of John F. Kennedy, "If I'm not having fun, then I'm not doing it right."

So if you can't laugh at yourself, you need to do some growing up and start doing it right. Now.

Innovation Teams: Stages of Group Development

Human beings are predictable, and so are groups of people. While no one can know exactly at any given time what a person or group is going to do, even the casual observer can tease out common trends and themes in human interaction. So let's look into the crystal ball of group dynamics and see what it has to tell us about the process of development of innovation teams.

Probably the best known description of the stages of group development was put together by a guy known to his mother as Brucey...and to us as B.W.Tuckman. After looking at over 50 group development models, he put forth the following four stages: 1) Forming, then 2) Storming, then 3) Norming, then 4) Performing.

Lesser known in the group dynamics world, but very well known in the Community (heart) Development world is M. Scott Peck's model: A) Pseudo Community, B) Chaos, C) Emptiness, and finally D) Community.

We think innovation teams fall somewhere between what we call a group and a community, and as we watch them develop, here's what we see.

PSEUDOTEAM:

Someone has called the group together and told them that they are to function as a team. Now by the time you've graduated from the eighth grade, you've got a pretty good idea of what a team is and how people are supposed to behave when they are on one. So that's what you do. You say nice things about the group. You make sure you don't rock the boat, even if you don't agree with something that others are saying or doing. You're very diplomatic as you put forth a proposal for thought or action. Why? Because you don't really trust these folks yet, and your "gator brain" is telling you "be careful Brucey, or they'll all gang up on you and eat you alive! Every group needs a scapegoat; make sure you're not it!" Correctly so, we are fearful of conflicting with the group. All of our nice statements about "what a great group of people this is" are really fostering a covert agenda. "Please, I promise not to say anything bad about you if you'll not say anything bad about me…together, we can all live happily ever after. Okay?"

BLAMESTORMING:

We are so interested in making sure that we don't get attacked by our group-mates, that the team will typically focus on blaming outside people and dynamics for the problem they have been given to solve. In this stage, the group will focus on the "poor us" energy as a way of bonding together. The problem is that hand wringers and finger pointers don't get the job done…and rarely get anything done. Additionally, it's not possible for humans working closely together to always avoid conflict with each other. Eventually, no amount of external blamestorming can cover up the fact that there will be tensions between members of the group. At this point, we typically see subgroups form within the team where the subgroup members blamestorm about how other individuals or subgroups within the team are the "problem." We're still trying to preserve our personal emotional safety here by finding at least a few allies within the team. Sadly, all too often, teams never progress beyond this point. The vast majority of "teams" that we observe and with whom we consult, are operating from this stage of group development.

If the group is to move beyond this stage in terms of its quality of performance it will occur in the following way: at some point in this storm, someone (or some critical mass of the group) will experience enough tension about the group's lack of effectiveness that they will begin to look for ways to take responsibility for moving the team forward on its agenda in a more effective way. This is a critical shift point in the formation since, as we'll later see, Innovation Teams are characterized by all of the team members taking responsibility, versus the more typical dynamic where only one or two people take up the task of leadership.

RESPONSE-ABILITY:

In innovation teams, (and this is critical) whether through training or very effective leadership or just the overall maturity of the group members, there is a shift of the entire group from looking outwards to fix blame, to looking inwards to fix the problem. *And not inward toward the team…inward toward themselves.* The question being asked by most (if not all) the team members at this time is something like "Okay, while all of the circumstances that we've been singing 'poor me' about are true, the only thing I have power over is me. What can I do to contribute my best to the effort of the team? What can I do to inspire the other team members to do the same?" Team members remind themselves that they have the ability to respond to their challenge in any way they want to, and that how they respond to the challenge will ultimately determine their success. The humility we've spoken of earlier is present just enough that the energy the member has put into judging others decreases and the energy for personal responsibility-taking increases.

Now, the gator brain hasn't gone away here, it still lurks, and here's a place where it's good that we have it. If enough group members are moving into the stage of Response-Ability, those that are a little slow to get there will sense that they are on the verge of being left out, and the gator fear that resides in their

---

Leading in Chaos

"Group process evolves naturally. It is self-regulating. Do not interfere. It will work itself out. Efforts to control process usually fail. Either they block process or make it chaotic. Learn to trust what is happening. If there is silence; let it grow; something will emerge. If there is a storm, let it rage; it will resolve into calm. Is the group discontented? You can't make it happy. Even if you could, your efforts might well deprive the group of a very creative struggle."

-- John Heider,
The Tao of Leadership

brainstem will often motivate them to shift up to a higher level of responsibility-taking. Being responsible becomes the norm of the group.

Inter-Depend-Dance:

How can I contribute my best to the team?

As the team members watch what they are doing in terms of group effectiveness (and they will because each is acting as if it is his or her job to grow the team…and it is every individual's job), a tremendous increase in trust of the team members appears. This trust sets up the group for two things. First, "I don't need to pay attention at such a high level to what you are doing, because I know you're taking responsibility for it and will handle your part. This allows me to focus on doing my part exceedingly well." Second, "when we're working together in a group and generating ideas to overcome various challenges, I know I won't be attacked for a less than perfect idea." The group dynamic is one of trying to get the best thinking on the table, and allowing for people's unpolished ideas to be a springboard for discussion of best possible ideas. It's a beautiful dance to watch and to be a part of. From a systems perspective, it's a lot easier to get to and maintain this level of productivity if there is some real mutual accountability for the delivery of some particular output from the group. Real accountability means that good output creates real positive consequences for all of the members, and that inadequate output creates real negative consequences for all of the group's members. In fact, a group can rarely be a team unless this system of pain/pleasure is in place.

Innovation Team:

Groups perform as an innovation team when in addition to the last two stages, they are also well trained in innovation skills. This is the difference between the typical high performance team, and one that is a notch above: the Innovation Team. You'll hear us say this again and again. Innovative thinking is a skill that can be strengthened at both the individual and group level. Innovation Teams are people who have taken responsibility to do the Inter-Depend-Dance while at the same time working diligently to increase their personal and group creativity skills. This is what makes them such darn fun dance partners…a multi-dimensional doe-si-doe!

Recap:

THE MOTTO: We're all human, and we all make mistakes. That's just the way it is. Get used to it.

Gator Brain: You can either respond to people around you like an alligator (eat, attack, run), or you can react like a thinking, feeling, human being and upshift to a higher level of being. Choose wisely.

The Myth of the Grown-up: Think you know everything? Think again. There are two types of people in the world: 1) People who are growing up and 2) Stuck people. Which one are you interested in being?

Humility vs. Arrogance: In group development, there are two approaches: 1) recognizing that an effective team needs to be constantly vigilant for non-productive behaviors and stop them immediately, and 2) an arrogant, cocky attitude that relies on past accomplishments as a way of making the team feel like they can accomplish anything…whether or not they're actually still able to.

The Value of Playfulness: Life's short. Why make it unpleasant? Just because the work is important doesn't mean that you have to take yourself seriously. Lighten up. It's not just more enjoyable, it also yields greater levels of innovation.

Stages of Innovation Team Development: All groups go through these stages if they are to become effective Innovation Teams:

> Pseudoteam: If they look like a team, they must be a team, right? Nope.

> Blamestorming: Not my problem. I didn't mess up. It's someone else's fault. Poor me!

> Response-ability : If we're going to do something, I have to take responsibility for making it happen.

> Inter-Depend-Dance: I can focus on doing my thing because I trust you to do your thing.

> Innovation Team : A high-performance team with skills for making innovation happen!

What are some places, situations, people, and problems that challenge you to manage your Gator Brain better?

What are some areas in your life in which you could do some more growing?

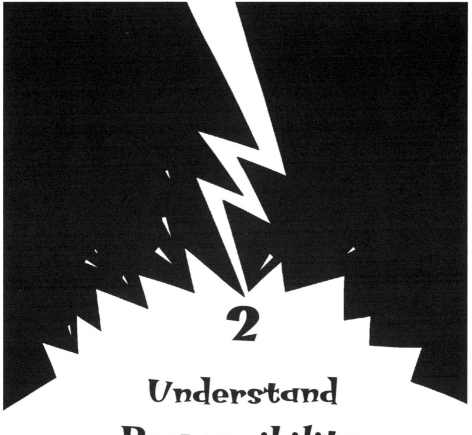

2

Understand Responsibility

"Whether you think you can or think you cannot, you're right."

- Henry Ford

"...the last of human freedoms [is] to choose one's attitude in any given set of circumstances, to choose one's own way."

-- Viktor Frankl

Get this: we create our personal reality. Now hang on…we're not saying that if a comet falls on your head you caused that to happen. We were watching, we saw it, and yup, a comet landed on your cranium and you did nothing to cause that. We're in agreement. But you…you have the option to make of that event anything you want. You could decide that you are having a very bad hair day, or that you now have the opportunity to wear that wig you've been fantasizing about. You could decide that you are the unluckiest person on the planet or that you have been chosen by the universe to receive a message: "Duck!"

The point is this: when you choose to become a victim of circumstance, your boss, a bad marriage, or assignment onto a crummy team…you lose your power. As soon as someone or something other than yourself is running the show in your head, you've lost your ability to do anything about it. So take back control. Get out of the twilight zone. Stop waiting for the things outside of yourself to change. Change the only thing you ever really can. You. Yes, you. Your thinking. Your perspective. Your opinions. Find a way of viewing the situation that puts you in the driver's seat. Now you can go where you can do something. Lead your boss. Be the spouse you want to have. Set the new standard of excellence on the team. Create the reality you want. It's all in how you focus your attention.

Who's the leader here?

When we're sitting and chatting with a group that is a high performance innovation team and we ask the question: "Who is the leader here?" the answer is always the same from every team member. "I am." Each member sees him or herself as the leader of the team. Everyone leads, all the time. Sometimes by making noise as the "mouth of the moment," sometimes by support, sometimes by strategic silence, sometimes by assertive challenge, but always with integrity and honesty. When every member is actively taking responsibility for the growth of the team and rapid movement on its mission, you'll see startling results. This is the true basis of the "entrepreneurial spirit" you hear people aspiring to.

Manage Your Thoughts

A lot of what we are suggesting be done to build innovation teams requires that the team members begin to master the skill

How to Practice Focusing Your Concentration:

1) Sit with good, open posture in a chair. Legs uncrossed, arms uncrossed.

2) Set a timer for five minutes

3) Focus your thoughts on something simple, such as:

> A simple, boring visual stimuli (e.g. a door knob, a spot on the wallpaper, an electrical outlet, etc.)
>
> A simple, boring sound (e.g. a fan, repetitive "New Age" music, street traffic, running water, etc.)
>
> A few words
>
> A simple repetitive phrase/ prayer/poem
>
> A simple physical sensation (e.g. your feet touching the floor, your hands on the arm of the chair, the breath entering and exiting your nose, etc.)

4) Whenever you notice your mind wandering from the focus, bring yourself back to the focus.

5) Don't beat yourself up for your mind wandering; just bring yourself back. Practice gentle mental discipline.

of turning their attention and thinking in directions that serve them. The word "mind" is derived from an Anglo Saxon word meaning "to pay attention to." We are thinking beings. We have minds and we can choose what we pay attention to. We're talking about mental hygiene skills here. Brain tuning.

Certain patterns of thinking move us forward toward innovation and success. Others hold us in place and increase the likelihood of failure. If we are going to defer judgment for instance, we need to have the ability to notice when the judge has slithered into our thinking and then change our thought pattern to one that is more productive. Just as an Olympic athlete sets aside any thoughts of an imperfect performance and replaces them with visualizations of perfection, so too must we quiet the judge when needed, and open to possibility thinking. We need to train ourselves so that our first reaction to newness is to look for possibility, not threat.

How do you get great at doing that?

The skill set needed is what we call "focusing your concentration." Essentially, in all of our exploration of this area of innovation and growth we have found only one pattern of mental training that works. While it takes many forms, the primary technique is to take time to attempt a simplification of your thinking. Here's how to do it: Focus your thought patterns on some simple thing, a simple visual stimuli, a simple sound or repetitive music, a few words, a simple repetitive phrase/ prayer/poem, a simple physical sensation (e.g. your feet touching the floor); and then, whenever you notice your mind wandering from the focal point, bring yourself back to it. Simple, no? Well…it is the practice of bringing yourself back which is the root skill for deferred judgment, which is simple, but difficult. When you're doing this, practice hearing and differentiating the voices in your head, then choosing which ones to turn your attention to at any given moment. Hearing the judge as it enters our consciousness, then setting that thinking pattern aside until later so that we might return to possibility thinking.

It's this same skill that is required for effective listening to others and we'll talk more about that later.

There is an added bonus. Stress is not what happens to you, stress is what you *think* about what is happening to you. Want to decrease your stress? Take responsibility to manage your thinking. Turn your attention away from the thought patterns that are getting you all worked up. Exercise your free will to perceive events in a way that works *for* you rather than *against* you. Innovation teams are filled with individuals exercising their will in directions that make their lives pretty wonderful. It's a big part of why they are great groups to work with.

There is another added bonus. According to the research of Candice Pert (the neurophysiologist who discovered the endorphin receptor site among others) and other brain researchers, the practice of consciously focusing your attention increases neuronal health in the pre-frontal cortex of our brain. And health in this area of our brain means the difference between good cognitive ability or dementia as we age. Want to have the maximum use of your brain for the longest time in your life? Want to be able to recognize who you are, where you are and who's around you when you are older? We bet you do. But it won't happen unless you exercise the prefrontal cortex.

So here is what we want you to do: find some way to practice focusing your concentration for at least five minutes every day. Challenge yourself to deal with the boredom of focusing all of your attention on a simple, boring sound, visual or physical stimuli, or thought. Choose something absolutely boring, and stick with it. Practice the mental discipline of returning to the "boring" thing whenever your mind wanders. If you can focus your attention where you choose when you're bored, you can focus your attention where you chose when you're

Why focus your concentration?

You'll listen better.

You'll be able to think more creatively.

You'll be able to defer judgement better.

You'll be able to work longer.

You'll maintain a better mood.

You'll stay healthier.

You'll communicate better.

You'll negotiate better.

Your sports will improve.

Your Gator brain will be more manageable.

agitated, judgmental, tired, angry, or whatever. Embrace the boredom. Become one with the boredom. Getting bored with this paragraph's repeated use of the word boring? Good. Pay attention. We'll talk more about this later.

How to Build a Better Idea Trap

We sit down at our desk, turn on our computer, open the word processing software and wait for the ideas to come to us. And wait. And wait. And then...nothing.

What happened to all those great ideas that were streaming and percolating through our heads while were drifting off to sleep? Where did those concepts go that were jumping like popcorn while we were in the shower? What happened to that million-dollar thought while we were driving to work? Gone. Back into the ether. Ever to be found again? Who knows?

If you've surveyed gajillions of people about where they are when they get their best ideas (and we have), you rapidly discover that a huuuuuuge percentage of people don't get their best ideas at their desks. In fact, almost nobody does. Rather the ideas come in bed, in the shower, in the car, during exercise, on a walk, at dinner, in the woods, in a mall, in a house, with a mouse, in a box, with a fox, in a boat, while you float, eating Green Eggs and Ham with Sam I am.*

So when the ideas come…wherever…the trick is to make sure those ideas don't escape. They're valuable ideas that come to you for free when you least expect it. And if you're prepared, you can capture the little scamps and use them later.

So carry a notebook with you. Capture them in your personal digital assistant. Use your pocket tape recorder. Write them on scraps of paper. Keep your laptop computer booted and ready. Whatever works for you, make sure you trap the ideas. Write them down. And be deliberate about saving, filing, or reviewing them on a regular basis.

Your ideas are your responsibility. So keep track of them like you would your cash. After all, ideas are gold. Treat them that way.

*With apologies to Dr. Seuss

Divergence and Convergence

Our brain has two basic phases during the innovation process. 1) generating ideas and 2) evaluating ideas. Most of the time, when we're innovating, we're doing both parts at the same time. First one then the other, immediately. You know the conversation.

Here's what it looks like when thinking about where to go for dinner.

Generating: We could go for Chinese food?

Evaluating: Nah, too much MSG.

Generating: How about Italian?

Evaluating: No, that will fill me up.

Generating: Perhaps the diner?

Evaluating: Not today, I'd like to avoid grease.

Generating: Well then maybe the burger place?

Evaluating: Nope, I had lunch there.

And so it goes. What happens to the generative side of the process is that it gets fed up with being rejected all the time. And that's just in our own brain.

Imagine when we add the entire team to the equation! Lots of ideas, lots of people shutting them down, and then eventually the group stops suggesting ideas and innovative thoughts.

One way to eliminate the idea shut down is to deliberately separate our generating from our evaluating. Otherwise it's like trying to drive with one foot on the accelerator while the other foot is on the brake. You'll make a lot of noise, you'll generate a lot of heat, you'll blow a lot of smoke, but you won't go anywhere. And according to Mr. Goodwrench, it's bad for the car.

It's easier said than done, so use these deliberate rules when you're generating and evaluating:

Guidelines for Generating: ✳✳

1) Defer judgment

You can judge the ideas all you want...LATER! For now, just keep them coming and write them down! Since you've been practicing focusing your concentration (see above), you'll notice when the judge appears and have the skill to turn your attention away from its blatherings.

2) Strive for quantity

Set a quota for ideas and don't stop until you get there. Even then, don't feel the need to stop generating! For simple issues, go for at least 30 ideas. More for complicated problems. When you generate lots of ideas, you'll get lots of great ideas. Quantity yields quality. Of course you'll get lots of bad ideas too, but you can deal with that when you start judging. Just not yet!

3) Seek wild and unusual ideas

Seek out wacky ideas. Actively try to find them. Because they stretch your mind. They force you to look in new corners of your brain where you'll find some odd ideas that might not be so outrageous when you tone them down a bit. It's easier to tame a wild idea than to invigorate a weak one.

4) Combine and build on other ideas

It's not enough to just generate a bunch of ideas unless you can build on them or fit ideas together that offer new possibilities. As you're generating, keep playing with ideas to see if you can let ideas spark off of each other to create new ones.

Guidelines for Evaluating:

1) Use affirmative judgment

Instead of pointing out all the ideas in which you don't see merit ("I hate that idea, and that idea, and that one, and that one, and that one. Wow, that one really sucks..."), focus on the ideas that are potentially valuable. Look for the good. Don't point out the bad. Never mind the ugly.

2) BE DELIBERATE

It's easy to see one idea and latch onto it, excluding all of the other great ideas that you generated. Watch out! Force yourself to be patient enough to explore each and every idea and ponder it's strengths before moving on to evaluate the next idea.

3) CHECK YOUR OBJECTIVES

As you evaluate ideas, remember what you're trying to accomplish. What was your original objective? Keep that in mind when you're reviewing ideas. Otherwise it's easy to go off on tangents without getting what you want. Like the saying goes, "When you're up to your butt in alligators, sometimes it's easy to forget that you started out to drain the swamp."

4) IMPROVE IDEAS

Not all ideas are immediately workable. Even promising ideas must be honed and strengthened. Use your discipline to take the time to improve ideas. Just because you're evaluating, doesn't mean you can't do a little generating on the side.

5) BE BRAVE: CONSIDER NOVELTY

When evaluating ideas it's too easy to fall back on the safe ideas you've tried before or that you know have been done before. But as we discuss elsewhere in this book, innovation generally doesn't come from golden oldies ideas. It comes from bold, fresh, new, novel ideas. And that's sometimes uncomfortable. So focus on looking for them.

If you can't remember all of that, remember this: to generate new ideas, you have to be able to defer judgment and open your mind to new ideas. And to evaluate new ideas, you have to open your mind to new ideas. Otherwise nothing gets through but old ideas. Now how innovative is that?!

**With thanks to Alex Osborn. From his book *Applied Imagination*

Pre-Judging Ideas:

How many of us are prejudiced? We don't mean prejudice in the sense of race, religion, gender, accent, clothing, size, or nose-hair. We're talking about the habit of judging new ideas before we have all the data. Remember what Sergeant Joe

Friday from Dragnet used to say, "Just the facts." Make this your motto before you evaluate an idea. Especially a new idea. The gator brain reaction to newness and innovation is to stomp it out. Pummel it. Smoosh it. Destroy it. And that's before it's been fully considered!

We can't emphasize enough how critical it is to judge ideas only when you have all the data. One way to do that is through a technique called POINt. We sometimes call it "Praise First." Here's how it works:

Pluses: What are (at least) three things you like about the idea?

Opportunities: What are (at least) three good things that might result if the idea were implemented?

Issues: What are some concerns you have about the idea (phrased as a question starting with "How to..." or "How might...")

New thinking: What are some ideas you have for how to fix the concerns? Brainstorm to answer some of the concerns that you noted in the previous step.

"Who the hell wants to hear actors talk?"

-Harry Warner, Warner Brothers, 1927

A subtle trick that occurs in POINt is that you are looking at the weak points of an idea by posing questions rather than listing complaints. You could list your concerns as a group of criticisms or complaints. The problem with that is that any brain within earshot will then begin looking for evidence to support the criticism. Idea-killing by avalanche if you will. It's just the way we're wired up…when you state a complaint to your brain in the form of a fact, your brain will look for evidence to support that fact. When we pose the concern as a question, we're pulling a fast one on our brain and all the other brains focused on the problem. When you ask your brain a question, it does everything possible to find an answer. It does everything possible to create a solution. Want some solutions? Phrase your criticism as a question. Because if you can't run a con job on yourself, what good are you?

New ideas look strange. They seem impractical. They make us feel uncomfortable, and they change the status quo. But they also unleash $15 quadrillion dollar industries. Think about all the technology that sits on your desk. The phone, the computer, the laser printer, the personal digital assistant (e.g. Palm V), the radio, the paperclip. At one time, they were all ideas that the inventors fought uphill battles to sell. All these inventors were told the ideas were crazy and would never work. The technology behind the Xerox copier took 25 years of research and $75 million to prove that it was commercially viable. If only some of those naysayers had used the POINt and avoided pre-judging the idea. The technology would still be on your desk, but some of those naysayers might be an awful lot more wealthy today.

Trick your brain with a question

Teams Don't Decide to Become Teams; Individuals Do

We've seen a lot of situations where a leader has said "We need to be a team." or "We work as a team here." And everyone waits around and wonders who is going to make that happen. Becoming a team is hard work in the first place; becoming an Innovation Team is harder yet. But the difficulty - and the work -- is at the individual level. The place where mind is. The group has no consciousness itself so can cause nothing to happen. A team is a group of individuals choosing to behave in particular ways. You can only observe a team. You cannot create it. All you can do is live the behaviors we are outlining in this book. And yes, you can and should challenge others to do the same. But you cannot cause them to do so. Only an individual can cause him/herself to behave and think in the ways we are describing. A team comes into existence when a critical mass of a group's members decide to behave as if they were a team. When everyone is doing that, you have a high performance team. When the members have developed the creative thinking skills and the group uses the various innovation tools we are describing here, you'll have an innovation team.

So hold yourself to as high a standard of thinking and behaving as you possibly can. You'll be making it easier for others to do the same, and as like attracts like, you'll end up being surrounded by folks who make it easier for you as well.

Everyone's the Leader

Who's the leader on an innovation team? If you've been paying attention, you might say "everyone." But that's not quite right. The team doesn't lead by consensus, rather it models leadership on an individual basis. Each individual is a leader and with that role comes tremendous responsibility. The responsibility to do the right thing, to model appropriate behavior, to think for the team, to take responsibility for making innovation happen as though no one else will, to hold to your convictions and to know when to let go and let others lead. On an individual basis.

Who's the leader? I am and you are, and he is, and she is. All at the same time. And when that's happening, there's no loafing, copping out, or sitting in the background. When it's happening, everyone is fully engaged in the process of making the team work and taking the actions towards greatness. What more could you ask for?

Yes we know this flies in the face of the "single leader out front" concept. The truth is that in single leader teams, it is the leader who is accountable for the output of the team, and the individual team members can easily hide from the leader. Sure, you can have a team that gets results in this style, especially if the leader is charismatic and an effective motivator. But then the quality of the team output is dependent on one individual. If the leader falters the team falls. In situations where the leadership is shared by every member of the group, a single individual's bad day or longer term life crisis doesn't derail the entire team's productivity. There are others ready to immediately step in and support the temporarily weaker contributor. And each of us is occasionally that person.

How to be a Leader

It doesn't take a fancy suit or a corner office, although sometimes it looks like it. It also doesn't take an election or a promotion or a raise. Or a title. Or a gold pen.

Howard Gardner, in his research on great leaders concludes that "Leaders provide leadership in two principle ways: 1) through the stories they tell and 2) through the kinds of lives they lead."

Want to be a leader? Be able to articulate your thoughts, wisdom, insight and opinions. Also model leadership by being the leader by whom you'd want to be led. Someone who has great insights and listens to others. Someone who knows what needs to be done and isn't afraid to get his/her hands dirty to make it happen. Someone who is great and recognizes and acknowledges greatness. Someone who is smart who knows when someone is smarter, no matter who he or she is. Someone who can articulate a vision and can follow one. Someone who knows the difference between right and wrong and isn't afraid to admit when they're the latter.

Leaders aren't great because they're told to be leaders or elected to be leaders. Leaders lead because they are leaders. Simple? Yes. Confusing? Yes, but needlessly. Try it this way: choose to be great, and people will follow.

Speeding The Team Development Cycle

So you've just found out that you're going to serve on an Innovation Team. The thing is, if you just found out, then the team is just forming. We can make some predictions about some things that are going to be happening so that you can move quickly to efficiently productive work.

Innovation Teams take time to grow. But you can fast track your development as a team by understanding the stages of team development, of which we spoke earlier (see "Innovation Teams: Stages of Group Development," at the end of "Surrender to Your Humanity" Chapter), assessing your team accurately for where it is, and then asking the right questions of yourselves to cause you to move forward as rapidly as possible into the realm of a high performance innovation team.

Remember, when you first get together, you're what we call a pseudoteam. You haven't done anything yet, and you probably wouldn't do much innovation even if you tried. There's not much trust at this point, and the good old gator brain is really clamoring to make itself heard at this stage of the process. Usually it'll play out in one of two ways for you. It may be saying "Take control, run this swamp!" Or, it's got you playing the game of swamp diplomacy, which sounds like this: "What a great group of people we are…I'm so privileged to get to serve on this team with all of you!" (This translates in cortex speak to "Please! I hate it when there is tension in a group…could we promise to stay away from any discussions which might raise conflicts?") The problem at this stage is that it's pretty tough to get any innovation work done. Innovation requires fairly high risk, high risk requires trust, trust requires incremental risk-taking, and even incremental risks create fear and tension.

Here's how it goes. Someone will take the risk to say something different than the overall thinking of the group. They'll introduce newness. When this happens, everyone's gator brain goes into hyper-vigilance mode to see what the behavior of their swamp mates will be. Will we all gang up on the deviant? If the group does, they'll be stuck at the stage called blamestorming until someone else deviates successfully to pull the group into their cortex.

The game of Swamp Diplomacy

Many groups never move past this stage. To be an innovation team - you must.

In emerging innovation teams, movement out of the blamestorming stage is caused by a critical mass of the group (most if not all members) choosing to manage their thinking in such a way as to empty out their own thoughts and preconceptions about "deviant" suggestions and give the gift of mind. Listening deeply to the others' thinking (we'll discuss this in more detail later). Something wonderful will emerge from this emptiness: innovative thinking.

At this point, assuming that the group has access to some of the other skill sets we've discussed (a big assumption to be sure), they become an innovation team in the real sense of the concept. Creating synergy by finding the innovation that exists in previously unconnected thoughts.

Using a dedicated process of formation, our experience is that about the fastest you can move from just "forming" to "high performance" is no less than three days and two nights. Our work with teams over the years has taught us that anything less is an insufficiently powerful rite of passage to cause these new patterns to "stick" in the minds of the members in a strong enough way to be able to keep the gators at bay. We're talking about off-site retreats with team development as the primary focus. We suggest that toward the end of the three days, you work on real work problems, but debrief your process for the quality of your teamwork rather than the quality of your product.

So ask yourself: "Am I behaving in the ways I need to in order to support this group to be a full fledged innovation team?" Don't accept "yes" for an answer. There is something that you can improve. Find it. Do it.

Mentoring New Team Members

Oh no, the team is going to change! We've got new blood coming into the group and we need to teach them how we run things here, because it works.

Not so fast. Instead of looking at it as a new team member joining, it's more appropriate to look at it as "re-creating the team." With people joining and/or people leaving, it's time to start all over again. Heck, there's a new leader in the team! (See "Everyone's the Leader") And the team isn't the same any more. Assuming that things will work the same way just because "most of us" are the same, or "we've still got the same name," is a mistake. Start all over again.

First, if your team has been operating pretty well, have the new team member read this book. Sure, that's a self-serving suggestion on our part, but you've got to start somewhere. (To order more copies, call…okay, now THAT's self-serving!) It's also very useful for new team members to read the following paragraph:

When we join a team that tells us (in some way) that it is an effective team, we generally take one of two positions, 1) that of the optimist or 2) the pessimist. If we're an optimist, then we're in a pretty good starting place because we turn our attention to seek data to support the team's contention that it is performing at a high state of function. And we'll find it.

If we're a pessimist, however, we'll have our "Crap Detectors®" out and operating at the highest level. With our detectors, we'll be looking for symptoms that the group is not all that it says it is. We'll look for symptoms of imperfection, and we'll find them because they're always present. If as a new member, we have not fully discarded the "Myth of The Grown-up" from our psyche, then we will need to judge the group's apparent imperfection, and use that judgment as a way of cutting ourselves slack for our own imperfections.

Regardless of whether we're an optimist or a pessimist however, we'll eventually see human imperfections in the members of the team. It is at this point that living by the principles we've been talking about becomes vitally important. Also at this point, having the basic language of Innovation Teams becomes so important because it allows the new member to dialogue effectively with the team members about the personal struggle of living the values of Innovation Teams. And it is this dialogue that signals the responsibility-taking that is the real entrance ticket to team membership.

There is an interesting dynamic that often happens with new members that can be VERY destructive if the new member is not watching out for it. Even in Innovation Teams, there can be dead wood. A member or two who are not pulling their weight. The team essentially works around this person because they are not taking responsibility and the team has exhausted its skills and energy to help that person do so. But because of some system issue, the person is still seen as a team member.

The truth is that in this case, the dead wood person will have a desire to find allies. They will have a sense of the lack of inclusion, even if it is unconscious. What better way to meet their social inclusion needs than to take the new team member under their wing. Yikes! Not a good thing.

Have a plan for inclusion

If you are that new team member, work to live up to the standard aspired to by the group, regardless of symptoms you might see that others are not living up to that standard. It's the right thing to do, and that should be enough reason to do it.

If you are a fully engaged Innovation Team member, take responsibility for spending time with and engaging the new member in the positive work of the team. And be careful to avoid the off-putting trap of arrogance. Nothing will drive a new team member away quicker than holier-than-thou energy from the established members of the team.

Bring All Your Power To The Team

Each of us has the opportunity to access subpersonalities and mental processes in our being in the form of what are called archetypes. Let's take a few moments to focus on the four primary archetypes shared by all human beings and ask you to do some thinking about how you might bring their power to the surface of your personality in a healthy and balanced way.

The four archetypes are:

> The King/Queen
> The Warrior
> The Magician
> The Lover

THE KING/QUEEN:

This is the part of us that has great concern for what happens in our realm. When there is pain in our kingdom, we experience it as our own. When there is joy, we feel that joy. Essentially, this is the archetype of connection. When we are accessing it, we are able to get inside the experience of the others in our realm. We have a paternal/maternal drive to create both joy and development in our "subjects." An Innovation Team member who accesses their King/Queen answers the question, "who's the leader" with the response, "I am." The member sees the purpose of the team not only as one of forwarding the business agenda it has been charged with, but also as being a rich place for the development of all of the team members.

Members who access this archetype ask themselves the question "How can I serve my teammates by helping them grow?"

THE WARRIOR:

This archetype has the energy that allows us to practice sensible self-denial in order to further our mission and that of the group. This is the part of us that bumps up against fear of failure or censure from the group and is able to reach out with some "Oh what the heck, go for it" energy. It is the part of us that acknowledges fear, but does not use fear as an excuse for inaction. It is the energy of courage and self-discipline.

The warrior has known failure, and because of this, has a sensibility that allows it to walk away from a challenge rather than fight to certain death. It enables us to retreat when the "enemy" is too strong and take a longer, more strategic view. Successful organizational culture change efforts, for example, require good access to the energy of the warrior. In the words of culture change guru Kenny Rogers, the warrior has to "know when to hold 'em, know when to fold 'em, know when to walk away, know when to run…"

Members who access this archetype ask themselves, "Is there any legitimate reason why I/we should be holding back?" and "How will I practice and improve my skills today?"

THE MAGICIAN:

This is the part of us that has skills and techniques to implement the desires of the king and warrior in an elegant, effective, and frequently subtle way. When we're listening well, sitting in silence as a strategy (as opposed to laziness), creating space for another's ideas, speaking persuasively or helping another to do so, we are utilizing the skills of the magician. The magician is the part of us that knows which tricks and techniques to use to get things to happen. When balanced with the King/Queen archetype it is never negatively manipulative.

The magician asks the question "What is the best, most efficient way to get this done?"

THE LOVER:

Yup, it's the place from which we access pleasure and energize others to do the same. It's the energy within us that says, "Let's enjoy this!" Innovation teams that have an ability to support each person's access to their lover are a lot of fun to be around. They openly admire the beauty that is synergy. They point out the funny stuff and bring laughter to the room. They reach out to each other with the message that it's good to take breaks and enjoy ourselves in this work. They affirm each other's work and communicate a sense of admiration to each other.

The lover wants to know "How can I make this a more pleasurable place to be and make sure we're all enjoying ourselves?"

BALANCE:

We suggest that each innovation team member work to achieve a balance of access to all of the archetypes. Lack of access makes for the Unconnected King/Queen, the Wimpy Warrior, The Incompetent Magician, and the Inept Lover. No thank you. The opposite extreme is to become possessed by an archetype and end up as a Tyrant, a Bully, a Manipulator, or a Pleasure Addict. These over- and under-attachments to the archetypes are called shadows, and it is commonly said that it's not a question of if you have shadows, but rather, "what are your shadows?"

Innovation Team members have surrendered to the fact that they have shadows, are working to overcome them and are attempting to bring the full balanced power of their archetypes to bear on the mission of the Innovation Team.

*With thanks to Robert Moore and Doug Gillette's "King Warrior Magician Lover"

Building Relationships

Everything that gets done in an Innovation Team is done through the quality of relationships that have been created with and among the individual members of the team. Your job as a team member is to work to build relationship between you and every other member of the team. As "the leader," it's also your responsibility to watch for others in the team who are in conflict, or not relating productively, with each other and work with them to fix that.

The concept here is to treat each other as friends.

We do nice things for our friends without necessarily being asked to do so. When we mess up and commit some social "indiscretion" with them we apologize with sincerity. When they mess up, we have the tendency to give them the "benefit of the doubt" and look for explanations that create an understanding of their error as something a little more complex than "s/he's a jerk." As Steven Covey notes, we make deposits into the emotional bank account more than we make withdrawals. We defend them when others run them down.

An Innovation Team, like any group of human beings, is a place with potential for conflict. The difference is that it ends more rapidly due to the team members living by three rules:

1) When I am out of relationship with someone on the team, I surface that feeling, look for causes in a non-blame atmosphere and fix the problem.

2) When someone comes to me with an issue with another teammate, I agree to listen if and only if the complainer will commit to work to resolve the issue, either alone or with my participation

3) As an Innovation Team member, I constantly strive to be a great listener. When an issue does come up, I apply my creative

How to act like a Friend on an Innovation Team:

1) Fix the problem, don't fix blame.

2) Agree to listen to complaints only if the complainer is committed to working to fix the problem.

3) Listen. LISTEN. And listen some more. Then look for solutions.

thinking and listening skills to come up with a solution that moves us forward and out of conflict.

Ultimately, an innovation team is only as good as its ability to leverage fully the experience and knowledge of its group members. Because of this, members work exceedingly hard to make sure personal baggage doesn't get in the way of the group's progress. They avoid the process of "blamestorming" and, when there is a problem, work to fix the problem rather than fix blame.

On-Demand Creative Energy

We all have our down days. Times when we'd rather stay in bed and just think about all of the things we'd like to have happen if we could just find the energy.

There is nothing wrong with recharging your batteries. We recommend it. We're not going to go to the grave with regrets for time not spent with our children, and adventures delayed until we're too old to live them. We're not going to die young from overwork (just ask our editor!).

We save time for our family and "other life" when we are highly productive during our working hours. So how can we make sure that we are? The trick is taking personal responsibility for managing our energy. There are three interwoven techniques for keeping energy up and available for when you need it.

Diet - We are what we eat. How's that for a brilliant new insight? The thing is, we don't always practice what we know about the dynamics of diet on our energy and thinking ability. Bottom line is this: Ingest for energy. That means maintaining steady blood sugar and neurotransmitter availability by eating a balanced diet that is generally richer in proteins and complex carbohydrates than what we typically eat and lower in fats and sugars. It means staying away from simple sugars, caffeine, and alcohol. All of our favorite vices. We reeaallyy wish we could tell you different, because then we could tell ourselves different, but we can't. Sorry.

Thought Control - We are what we think. Sure, we know we
just contradicted ourselves…but we think you'll understand.
If you keep turning your attention to how tired you are, you'll
make yourself more so. It's possible to a large extent to will
yourself to alertness. A lot of our mental vacationing at work
is simply self-indulgence…cut through the crap.
Are you really tired? Or just unmotivated? It's the
job of the leader to motivate you, right? And
who is the leader of your Innovation Team?
That's right. You! So crack the whip or send
yourself on a vacation, but get out of the twilight zone.

Posture and Movement - Our body and mind are connected.
Neurologists like Candice Pert (remember, the neurophysiologist who discovered the endorphin receptor site) are now saying that the seat of our consciousness is not just in our
brain…they're beginning to use the term "bodymind." We get
a lot of pleasure from pointing out Descartes error when he
asserted that "What is of the body is not of the mind, and
what is the mind is not of the body," It's just not so. The most
rapid technique we know of to increase your energy is to change
your posture. Sit up! Stand tall! Look alert! Walk like you are
on top of the world looking down on creation and the only
explanation you can find…(oh sorry, lost it for a moment).
Change to an alert posture and your brain starts cooking again.
Stuck for an idea in the meeting? Stand up, put your hand to
your chin, put a furrow in your brow, and act like the wise one.
Wise thoughts (or at least energizing wise cracks) will rapidly
follow.

We don't really need more hours in the day and more energy
than we have (although some days it would be welcome); we
just need to manage ourselves so that we're cooking along in
creative style. The energy will come in the doing.

How to Motivate People to be More Creative

Want to motivate people to be really creative in a great way?
Forget about rewards and threats. They won't do it. Theresa
Amabile, a professor at Harvard, has conducted lots of research that consistently shows that creativity and innovative
ideas come from inside, and are motivated from within by
personal desire. While it is possible to generate some creativity
by offering money, positions, competition, threats, and pun-

ishments; these external forces are not nearly as effective as the desire to be more creative for our own internal reasons.

Dr. Amabile's research is very clear: creative products created by people motivated by extrinsic forces aren't nearly as creative as those created by people who were intrinsically motivated.

So here's what you need: people who really want to do a great job, who are clear about their desire to make something creative happen. People who want to move the team forward with their innovation because it's what they want to do. Want great results? Create a team of people who really want to create great results. Not because they have to or because they're forced to, but because it's what they want.

Need more research? Try this: according to Dr. Goran Ekvall of the University of Lund in Sweden, 67% of the statistical variance accounted for in the climate for creativity in organizations is directly attributed to the behavior of the leader.

Huh?

Let's simplify: If things are going right, there's a 67% chance that it's the leader's doing. If things are going wrong, there's a 67% chance that it's the leader's fault.

Once again, who's the leader? Right. You are. Still believe that one person can't make a difference? Sorry, but you do make a difference! So if you want great results, work to create a team of people where great results are wanted, welcomed, and strived for. Then provide support, resources, encouragement, hard work, and stay out of their way!

Want to motivate people to be creative? Enlist them in your vision and foster an honest desire to create innovation. That's where the greatness is.

The Art and Science of Focused Concentration

Earlier, we spoke about managing your thoughts (See "Manage Your Thoughts" in this chapter). We want to explore that subject just a bit more here. Slightly repetitive are we? You got us! Why? This subject is hugely important and what we know about learning is that repetition is the parent of both skill and knowledge. And each time we say it, we add another layer. Read on:

Mental focus, visualization, contemplation, positive thinking, guided imagery, powerthinking, meditation, the zone, prayer in the Holy Spirit, progressive relaxation, self-hypnosis, chanting, breathwork, tantra, tai chi, reflection, trancework, alpha state, astral travel, sitting zazen, oogliboogly, whatever makes this a subject you might be willing to explore, you call it that.

We'll call it "focusing your concentration."

Why we want you to be good at it is that it's a key to generating lots of innovative thinking and of keeping the judge at bay when you are generating ideas. It's the entire skill set of managing your thinking to reduce stress. It's THE skill for making sure you are maintaining thoughts that connect you to others and keep the gator brain in the non-evolved evil murky swamp where it belongs.

How you do it doesn't really matter, but here's the process that seems to underlie just about all of the techniques we have explored (and we've explored a lot of them). Try to think about one simple positive thing and nothing else (the movement of air in and out your nose, your children's names, a holy word or phrase, a simple sound…)

You won't be able to do it.

But trying causes you to notice the thoughts that are flowing through. When you do, notice that they're there and gently let them go, even if they're fun, returning back to your focal point until you notice the next cluttering thought and release that and so on…Do this for at least five minutes every day or up to twenty minutes if you want to get really good at it. The practice helps you get good at shifting your thinking from one place to another…and that's the key to searching your psyche for innovative ideas and quieting the judge when it appears. It's the way you energize your innovative brain.

Recap:

THE MOTTO: I can react to anything however I want. So I'm going to make the reaction a good one!

Manage Your Thoughts - Want to think/create/evaluate/ negotiate/concentrate better? The secret is in learning to manage your thoughts by practicing "focused concentration" every day.

How To Build A Better Idea Trap - Ideas come when - and where - you least expect them. Have a system in place to capture and record them.

Diverging And Converging - When searching for innovative solutions, the least effective way is to generate and evaluate simultaneously. Want twice as many ideas that are twice as good? Separate your generative and evaluative thinking. That goes for you and your team.

Pre-Judging Ideas - Discarding ideas before you've thoroughly evaluated them is wasteful. Okay, dumb too. So make a practice of evaluating ideas/concepts/suggestions with the POINt tool. What are the pluses of the idea? What are the potential opportunities that might result? What issues or concerns (phrased as questions) do you have? Overcome the concerns by brainstorming some new thinking to fix them.

Teams Don't Decide To Become Teams; Individuals Do - Waiting around for "the team" to make it happen is like waiting to win the lottery. Without buying a ticket. It ain't gonna happen! Only the individual members of the team can make it happen. One at a time. By their own choice.

Everyone's The Leader - Don't wait for others to lead. It's up to you. All the members of an Innovation Team answer, "I am" when asked, "Who's the leader?"

How To Be A Leader - "Choose to be great and the people will follow." Be great and you will do great things. It really is that simple.

Speeding The Team Development Cycle - Being aware of the stages of Innovation Team development will get you to high performance innovation if you deliberately do the hard work of getting through blamestorming quickly. You can't escape it, you can only work through it.

Mentoring New Team Members - New team members happen. And they need to be integrated into the team and made to feel like fully contributing members of the team right NOW. What can you do to help that?

Bring All Your Power To The Team - Be aware of the archetypes of leaders: King/Queen, Warrior, Magician, Lover. By balancing these essential ways of being, you can contribute to the Team in a healthy and productive way.

> Kings/Queens ask themselves the question "How can I serve my teammates by helping them grow?"
>
> Warriors ask themselves, "Is there any legitimate reason why I/we should be holding back?" and "How will I practice and improve my skills today?"
>
> The Magician asks the question "What is the best, most efficient way to get this done?"
>
> The Lover wants to know "How can I make this a more pleasurable place to be and make sure we're all enjoying ourselves?"

Building Relationships - We build Innovation Teams by behaving in the same way that friends behave. Here are three rules:

> 1) When I am out of relationship with someone on the team, I surface that feeling, look for causes in a non-blame atmosphere and fix the problem.
>
> 2) When someone comes to me with an issue with another teammate, I agree to listen if and only if the complainer will commit to work to resolve the issue, either alone or with my participation.
>
> 3) As an Innovation Team member, I constantly strive to be a great listener. When an issue does come up, I will apply my creative thinking and listening skills to come up with a solution that moves us forward and out of conflict.

On-Demand Creative Energy - Diet, Thought control, Movement and posture. These are three things that determine our energy level. By focusing on positively managing these areas in a healthy way, we ensure a peak energy level for maximum creativity. So stay away from the fried pork rinds when you need creative energy!

How To Motivate People To Be More Creative - Okay, you can't. You can only help people discover their motivation since internal motivation is the most effective way to get people to innovate.

The Art and Science Of Focused Concentration - It doesn't matter what you call it, just spend time every day practicing the management of your thoughts…it's the most effective way to get that innovative brain of yours cranking out ideas!

3

Conscious Listening,
Clear Speaking

"A team of giants needs giant pitchers who throw good ideas. But every great pitcher needs an outstanding catcher. Without giant catchers, the ideas of giant pitchers may eventually disappear."

-- Max DePree, *Leadership is an Art*

You only have your own experience to draw upon at any given moment. One of the most efficient ways to expand your range of experience is to get inside the experience of others. Yes, we're saying, "Live vicariously" when so many others seem to be saying only, "Get out there and experience the world directly instead of just reading it in a book." While we also agree with that, you can't do everything, so we're making the case that we've listened to the Hemmingway message for so long we've forgotten just how valuable it is to be really skilled at getting inside the experience of another by just listening. And how important it is to master the art of telling the story so that others have the benefit of our experience and wisdom. The thing is, we need to work to master both skills and constantly ask the question about our personal balance between yapping our trap and lending our ear.

There is a great American idiom that goes: "Children need to mind their parents." Our take on that is that if a child would allow a parent's thinking and wisdom to occupy their mind -- if the child would allow the parents thoughts to be their thoughts -- they would exhibit the behaviors and attitudes that the parent is attempting to help them learn. It's the same in all of our relationships. We need to be so skilled in listening and speaking that we create space in our mind for other people's thoughts and place our thoughts in the mind of the other with accuracy and delicacy. Lacking the skill of the (fictional) Vulcan Mind Meld® popularized on the TV show Star Trek, this is the best we can hope for.

But when we do this well…oh, the things that happen! Innovation occurs in the space of previously unconnected thought forms.

Members of Innovation Teams are folks who have successfully challenged themselves to learn to listen and listen to learn. They trust that the other is doing the same thing (and if it's an Innovation Team, they are) so there is no need to spend their listening time occupying their mind with a rehearsal about their own upcoming speech. They are "minding" their teammate. And to our way of thinking this is one of -- if not the greatest -- gift you can give another person. If all we are is thought, when we allow another's thoughts to be our own for a while, we are giving them all that we are. Innovation teams are places of huge synergy and huge trust precisely because of their ability to listen consciously and speak clearly.

**Mind
your
team-mates!**

In the words of a quote attributed to Mahatma Gandhi, "Live as if you were going to die tomorrow. Learn as if you were going to live forever."

The Subtle Truth About Active Listening

Have you ever been trying to get a point across to someone and they say something to you like "I hear what you're saying?" And you know that they haven't a clue. Yuck. There's no listening going on here at all, and in fact, that kind of listening (as in they're "kind of" listening) weakens the relationship rather than building it.

Active listening requires that the listener paraphrases what the speaker is saying and checks in from time to time to find out if they are hearing it right. For two reasons.

The first, and the most obvious, is that understanding the other's point of view is what it takes to create together and to find the synergistic ideas that exist in the arena of previously unconnected thoughts. More on that .

The second, and the more important from the perspective of team dynamics is that when you correctly paraphrase someone's thoughts back to them, they feel well heard, and relationships are strengthened. It is a great compliment to another when your listening behavior is saying, " I value your thoughts enough to spend some real mental energy making sure I really understand what you are saying."

It's not good enough however, if you are sure only in your own mind that you understand what the other person is saying. The relationship is built most effectively when the speaker is absolutely sure, based upon paraphrasing, that they are being fully understood.

Now the truth is that it's hardest to do this, yet of the most value, when you and the other person are in conflict. Listening requires someone to have the mental discipline and emotional maturity to shut up. And somebody has to go first. Usually it's the leader. And just who is the leader on an Innovation Team? Umm…if you don't know by now, you haven't been paying attention (hint: it's YOU).

Innovation Team members take the time to listen actively. So what do you hear us saying?

A Word About Body Language

A lot has been written in the business and human dynamics literature about the way that our body language augments what we are saying and how it offers a clue to what we are really feeling. You can attend seminars to learn how to modify your own posture and body language in such a way as to get into rapport with someone, or to manipulate their perspective of you as someone who is trustworthy.

Our attitude about the dynamics of body language in Innovation Teams is this: If you are looking for the good in your teammate, if you are truly curious about what they are saying, if you respect them, and you have some personal humility when you are in conflict, then your body language will naturally fall into a posture that supports the work of better relationships and more effective innovation dynamics. When other authors say, "pay attention to your body language" they're missing the bottom line: Pay attention to your thoughts; the body will follow.

Openness is the posture of genius!

It is true, however, that you can manipulate yourself with your body language. If you notice that you're tensing up and crossing your arms in conflict, force yourself to relax and be in an open posture, not to "hide" your disagreement from the other, but to precipitate different thought patterns in your own mind. Open posture yields open thinking, a relaxed body allows for relaxed consideration of multiple viewpoints. If you're having trouble understanding something someone is saying, check your posture. Make sure your arms and legs are uncrossed. If you're seated, sit up and lean forward attentively. Use your entire "bodymind." Only then can you really say you gave it your best shot.

The Art of Apology

Since you are a human being, you can count on making misteaks and doing things that hurt others in some way. Assuming you have developed your sense of connection to them, you're prob-

How to Apologize:

1) Genuinely feel bad about what you've done. If you're not really sorry, and can't understand why they're upset, think about it and come back later.

2) State clearly what you did wrong.

3) Communicate how you think the other person might feel given their experience of what you did. Try to understand their experience.

4) Say you're sorry.

5) Listen to them vent if they need to.

6) Say you're sorry and make a genuine commitment to making sure you don't commit the offense again.

7) Ask for them to accept your apology.

8) BONUS STEP - Go out for ice cream

ably going to feel bad for doing whatever dastardly thing you did.

Good.

But that's not enough. You need to apologize.

There are effective and ineffective ways to apologize. Think about why you're doing it…you want the other person to really understand that you feel crummy about what you said, did, or didn't do. You want to get back into relationship with them as soon as possible. While you can never control fully what their reaction to your apology will be, you can increase the odds that you will move beyond this limiting dynamic in your relationship and get back to the joy of synergistic innovation.

The first rule is this: don't apologize if you don't really feel a sense of chagrin. False "I'm sorrys" are seen through for what they are, even if the other person doesn't say so. Generally they're a cover-up for a statement that loosely translates "Anybody else would have done the same thing in this circumstance and you're kind of a jerk for getting upset with me about it." A real relationship builder, wouldn't you say?

If you are taking responsibility for your offense, then the place to start is with a clear statement of exactly what you did and a description that communicates your understanding of what the other person might feel given their experience of what you did. In other words, put yourself in their shoes for a moment. Then you say that you're sorry for having caused that, and if they need to vent for a bit, you listen and follow their venting with another "I'm sorry" and whatever commitment you honestly feel you can make to prevent the offense from occurring again. For maximum satisfaction, ask the other person if they accept your apology. This will make you both feel better…assuming they accept your apology! And if they don't, it's time to either listen again or give them some time.

What? You want a magic formula to make life easy? Sorry. Not here. Call us if you find it.

The Use Of Intuition

What? Are we crazy? Listening with intuition? What are these guys going to say next, that Innovation Teams should have a Psychic on call ("Hello, Innovation Team Psychic hotline…")?

So just what is intuition anyway?

Most people agree that "intuition" is knowing something accurately without consciously understanding why you know it. The fight starts when we try to define where the information comes from. There's no end to theories and opinions about the where and the how, and frankly, that's a minefield of passionate opinion that we are not willing to walk into. Call us cowards…or just plain smart.

However, we are willing to put a stake in the ground and take the position that intuition does exist, and is a useful addition to the innovative process if we consciously attempt to access it and use it in our decision-making. Intuitive ideas seem to surface when we carry a question in the back of our head about a problem we are working on and when we are willing to find answers that come to us by way of seemingly unrelated metaphor and imagery.

Say what?

Listen to your dreams, Bucko, and ask yourself what ideas are coming to you by way of the imagery and storyline. Pay attention to the songs that seem to run through your thoughts almost unbidden during the day…what are the lyrics that your thinking is telling you. Allow yourself to think about nothing every once in a while and see where your thinking takes you. Take some time out to do a focused concentration activity. Great ideas often pop up when you stop looking for them. Doodle for a bit, and look at your doodle after you've finished…now why did you do that doodle? Survey your body. Are there feelings or sensations that seem to be telling you something?

The bottom line is this: Innovation Team members take data from anywhere they can get it. Intuition is one of those places.

We're not sure why we put the preceding section in here, but somehow it seemed right.

Abandon your Problem

Einstein did it. So did Edison. And Mozart. So what can we learn from some of the greatest minds the planet has ever seen? Simple. When the pressure to generate ideas is great, but the ideas are not,

walk away from the problem either literally or figuratively. We will now tell you where to go:

Do some quick exercise (20 pushups)

Go home

Leave the problem alone for an hour, a day, or a week

Take a lunch break

Better yet, buy us lunch!

Just remember to bring your notebook with you to record the idea when it comes...because it will arrive when you least expect it!

Incubation: The Value of Doing Nothing

It was Graham Wallas, in 1928, who put the term "incubation" into play: Such an important sounding word for something so easy to do: walk away from your problem. Wallas described four basic stages that a person goes through when generating ideas:

1) Preparation - learning as much about the particular problem as possible by gathering data, checking facts, exploring emotions, and/or clarifying what is the problem or issue.

2) Incubation - walking away from the challenge for a while to do something else, with the intention of letting the mind subconsciously process the issue.

3) Illumination - the legendary "Aha!" of creativity...getting the idea, the flash of inspiration, the jolt of knowing that you've generated a brilliant solution.

4) Verification - checking to make sure that the brilliant idea is, in fact, brilliant, and not just gas. It's doing the research to make sure you're right, checking with others to see if they understand, or perhaps building a prototype for future exploration.

Of Wallas' stages, it's the second one that's less valued or understood. The other stages are incorporated in various problem-solving models including the scientific method, but incubation? Not so much. Really, when was the last time your supervisor told you to do something else while s/he was waiting for your brilliance? How many times have you been rewarded for not being in your office? What is the typical reaction when you're discovered surfing the web at your desk?

Once upon a time, the pace of business and life was such that taking time to think about things was part of life. We worked shorter hours, didn't have the option of e-mailing ideas, answers and solutions out Right Now. It wasn't possible. The excuse of "it's lost in the mail" was always available, and frequently accurate. The pattern was such that we had time to mull over ideas while the proposal was in the typing pool, or during a real lunch HOUR, or while we went home rather than burning the proverbial midnight oil.

But think about it, where are you when you get your best ideas? The responses are typically things like, "in the car," "on the boat," "at the coffee shop," "in the outdoors" or "taking a shower." Rarely does anyone say, "at work" or "at my desk." How about you? If you're like the vast majority of the people we talk with, you're not getting great ideas where you're supposed to be getting them.

There are legendary stories that prove that some of the world's greatest ideas were illuminated at odd times. Einstein came up with his greatest theories while canoeing, walking or sailing. Edison, a man with 1,093 patents to his credit, would go down to the dock and fish (or at least pretend to) when he was stumped. The discovery of the structure of benzene happened during a dream. Mozart exercised in order to get un-stuck when working on his symphonies and concertos.

In short, let your mind work on the problem while you're thinking about something else. Let your mind noodle on the idea while you're eating pasta. Allow yourself to bake the idea while making cookies. Put the brain on "spin" while doing laundry. Literally sleep on the problem. Just don't think about it…at least not consciously.

IMPORTANT: whatever you do, or wherever you go, make sure you take a notepad with you, or something else to capture brilliant ideas. Great ideas will come to you when you least expect it. The illumination, which follows the incubation, is unpredictable. And temporary. Capture the idea while it's available, because when you get back to the office, it might be gone AND forgotten. And then you're back at square one. But if you capture the idea, then you too can be a creative hero!

Work on something else
Go run an errand
Do a routine task
Run the stairs
Go say hello to a friend
Check your e-mail
Go get a beverage
Return a phone call
Work on your expense report
Go outside for some fresh air
Stretch

The Value of the "Gut Check"

Our favorite graffiti of all time was spray-painted on a garage door on Main Street in Buffalo, NY. It said, "Validate subjectivity." Funny, when you think about it. Dumb if you don't think about it.

Yet it's something that we do every day. We ask, "Which is the best?" "What is the 'right' answer?" "What are the appropriate criteria for the decision?" "What do the experts say?" "What

do our customers say?" "Where's the research on that?"

On a regular basis, we do research (both formal and informal) to get the answer that we really want. The answer that exists in our gut. What, deep down, we really want. Ever find yourself in a quandary and you ask one friend after another what they would do until you find one that tells you what you want to hear? Of course not. But you know other people who do that. All the time.

What's staggering is that the cultural analysts* will tell us that the bigger the decision (e.g. what kind of car to buy, which house to purchase, whom to marry), the less likely you are to use objective criteria. Consider a product which:

> "Honey, I can't find the owner's manual..."

Has no owner's manual

Cannot be returned

Is extremely expensive

Has no warranty

Is prone to breakdowns

Requires maintenance 24 hours a day for the first years of ownership

Causes physical and emotional pain

Leaks regularly

Consumes household resources

Expands in size over 600% at an unpredictable rate

Why the hell would anybody want one of these? Or who would actually make these contraptions? Good question. But you're reading this because at least two people did. We're talking of course about a baby. Think about it. There is a huge objective rationale against having a child, yet a vast majority of couples and singles capable of having children have at least one! How could that be?!

Bottom line is that we're really driven by our "gut." By our intuition and internal programming. By our beliefs and attitudes. Not by what necessarily makes sense objectively. The fastest growing segment of the automobile market as we write this is the Sport Utility Vehicle category. You know, the huge four wheel drive station wagons. In fact, there's an increasing likelihood that you own at least one. Yet how many people actually make use of the capabilities of these extremely tough off-road vehicles? Less than 5% of SUV owners ever take these off-road vehicles off-road. Sure, they're great in the snow.

So how come there are so many of them in Southern California?! Yes, they carry lots of cargo, but so do mini-vans and station wagons, and much more efficiently!

Fact is that we buy cars and other high-ticket items based on what we want, not what we need. And most people don't want minivans until they discover how versatile they are. If you stop to look at how much this creeps into our business decision-making, it's a bit unnerving. We couch it behind "experience," "qualitative research," "what I hear," and "our customers don't know what they want." Our brains are amazing processing units, as are our guts. Objectivity? There's really no such thing. But it's easier to say than "validated subjectivity."

So is it bad that we use our "guts?" Absolutely not. Unfortunately, most of us don't like to admit our reliance on our "gut check," and many of us try not to be dissuaded by it. We believe it's one of the great unspoken truths of business. We make decisions based on our guts but don't admit it. The fact of the matter is that it exists, and there's nothing we can do about it.

Better yet, embrace it; realize how powerful it is and how amazingly wise it is! Use it! Listen to it! Voice it. Share it. At the very least, it will provide an interesting point of view. Okay, so the majority of us might not opt for a child if we thought it through objectively. Instead we'd hire someone to cut the grass and wash the dishes. We'd do the aunt/uncle thing when we wanted to see something cute. But if it weren't for people making the decision to have children, none of us would be here.

Which would make the world a pretty lonely place. And all those Sport Utility Vehicles and mini-vans would just be parked on the side of the road. Rusting in peace.

*With thanks to Margaret King and Jamie O'Boyle of Cultural Studies & Analysis.

Style Differences in Team Members

Brace yourself. We're going to rock your world with this amazing factoid: people are different. No! Yes, it's true!! And while we may know that intellectually, sometimes it's hard to be actively conscious of it when someone we're working with (or trying to work with) is acting in a way that is opposite of the way that we would act. Or think. Or be.

There are so many different ways to access personal style. There are so many different dimensions of it that we can go crazy trying to figure out just how different or similar people are. Consider just some of the different ways of looking at personality differences:

> Extrovert vs. Introvert
>
> Paradigm strengtheners vs. Paradigm breakers
>
> Fact-deliberators vs. Implementers
>
> Thinkers vs. Feelers
>
> Rule makers vs. Rule breakers
>
> High energy vs. Low energy
>
> Auditory vs. Visual
>
> Kinesthetic vs. Cerebral
>
> Experiential vs. Vicarious
>
> Public displayers of affection vs. Private types
>
> Lovers vs. Fighters
>
> Masculine Culture vs. Feminine Culture
>
> Bathroom readers vs. non-bathroom readers
>
> Crumplers vs. Folders

We all know that there is no one right way to be, right? Even if you are an Introverted-paradigm-strengthening-implementing-feeling-rule-making-low-energy-audidory-cerebral-vicarious-public-displayer-of-affection-fighter-who-reads-in-the-bathroom, there is at least some value to other perspectives. Yet it's so easy to find ourselves frustrated by people who, for whatever reason, don't see it the way we do. They insist on doing it their way and we insist on doing it our way and tension results.

One of our former bosses used to want to know everything about the situation, while we were busy suggesting strategies to be implemented. One of our former colleagues needed to see all ideas in writing before making a decision, while we hated "wasting" the time to write the memo. Were they wrong? No. Were we wrong? Of course not.

Yet there is friction between the styles. Until we realize what's going on. When we realize that we're bumping up against differences in style, then we can actually make headway on moving forward in working together productively. When you and the other person can become aware of the style differences, then you can begin to lubricate the friction by cooperating in helping the other person work in their preferred style while you work in your preferred style to become more and more effective in your work together. Look out Innovation Team, here we come!

Creating Different Perspectives on the Team

Just as different styles on a team have the potential of causing friction, so too do these style differences offer the possibility of profound insights and discoveries. Imagine the power of two people with opposite ways of doing things approaching a task, compared to two people with the same way of looking at it. Which will create new insights? Which will create synergies never seen before?

There's huge opportunity potential in having people get new insights by looking at things in new and different ways. One way to make this happen is to pair up opposites on a project. Or to make sure that for every yin in the group there's a yang. Jerry Hirshberg of Nissan Design International hires car designers in pairs who are very different in order to generate creative tension.

Another way to do that is to assign "roles" to team members: designate a provocateur, a rule-finder, a heretic, a synthesizer, an organizer, a disrupter, or whatever function is needed to shake up the group. Either through disruption or through synthesis. By messing things up or tidying things. By drawing pictures or putting them into words.

Ask your team, "What are we good at?" More important, ask yourselves, "What don't we do well?" By focusing on what are the deficits, you can begin the process of actively searching out ways to compensate for them. That could mean a new person or someone who is responsible for paying attention to that deficiency...for a day, for the week, for the duration of the project. Not only will that cause growth for the team, but also for the person. Sounds like a bonus!

Phrase Problems as Questions to Put Problems in Jeopardy

Pop quiz time. Which problem is easier to solve:

A) We have no money

B) In what ways might we obtain funding?

If you've sussed us out at all, you'll know that the answer is "B." Why? Because our brains love challenges. We're driven to find the answer to questions. On the other side (lobe?), our brains don't like obstacles. And in fact our brain seeks to validate that the obstacle exists. Putting a barrier in front of us leads to a sense of defeat, which creates resignation to the way things are. "Darn, we have no money. I guess it's over." As opposed to John Belushi's famous inspirational speech from Animal House, "It's not over until we say it's over." And the best way to make it happen is to phrase the problem as a question.

Starting problems with four simple phrases automatically signals our brains, and the brains of the others on the team, that we need a solution. So start thinking, brain! Here are the magic "statement starters" to get you unstuck:

How to...

How might...

In what ways might...

What might be all the...

No money? Instead of lamenting the fact that you're cashless, try looking at it as "How might we obtain funding?" Or "How might we reduce expenses." Or, "In what ways might we leverage what we have?" Or "What might be all the ways to raise more money?"

Think that will help to spark some ideas from a smart, well-functioning, creative brain (like yours)? You betcha!

The Power of the Agenda

In order to really get into the mind of another person, it is important to understand what they want you to understand, or to be clear about what you want them to understand about you. Especially when working together in a team. How many possible conversations do you think are going on in the heads of the members of an Innovation Team?

A great technique for harnessing the focus and concentration of a group is to be very explicit about where the conversation will go. Craft an agenda that is a clear statement of the topics to be addressed, so that everyone can focus.

There are three key elements of a good agenda:

> Purpose
>
> Process
>
> Outcome

A fourth element, which is frequently helpful for running group meetings, is "Timing." Here's how they work:

PURPOSE:

Identify for the team (or the other people in the conversation) why it is that you are having the conversation. Is it to share information? To generate ideas? To reach team consensus? And about what? Be specific. Be direct. Be as explicit as you possibly can.

PROCESS:

How are you going to accomplish your purpose? Are you going to brainstorm? Will there be a vote? Is it going to be a free-ranging discussion? Perhaps you'll all go to the library to divide out research. Maybe a walk.

OUTCOME:

What is it that you want to walk away with? What is your desired outcome? A list of possible ideas? A plan of action? A commitment from group members to chip in a billion dollars each? Be specific, don't hold back, and don't let there be any surprises.

TIMING:

If you're running a meeting with a limited time frame (when is there unlimited time?), you'll need to be deliberate about setting a time limit or guideline, and then sticking to it. It's harder (although very possible) to run out of time when you're deliberate about how much time you are willing to allocate to a specific task. Got three things to accomplish in an hour? Each one receives twenty minutes? Halfway through the meeting, if you're not on topic number two, you know you're in trouble and you need to reconfigure either the agenda or the conversation.

We've seen so many conversations go nowhere because of expectations that didn't mesh up. People then get frustrated, angry, uncooperative, and gator-like. Creating the agenda in advance helps avoid that and will help to make sure that everyone gets their needs met, or at least realize that if they don't get them met today, they will at a defined time in the future.

Listening Completely

Huh? Oh, sorry.

It's been said that in order to have a really productive conversation, we first need to understand what's being said, and only then make sure that we are understood. It's been called "talking with your ears," "understanding the situation," and "listening from nothing." And gosh, is it effective.

And difficult.

Ever try to have a conversation with someone about something that's a little bit, shall we say, dicey? Even though you walked into the conversation with the best of intentions, before you knew it you were arguing, raising your voice, saying the same thing again and again and wondering why the other person was such a...how to put it nicely...close-minded idiot?

It's very easy to do, and we blame it on our gator-brain (although the temptation is to blame it on your gator-brain, but that just proves the point that it's our gator-brain talking). We get caught up in the fact that there is a difference of opinion, or that they want to focus on something else, or that it has great taste, yet they insist on saying it's less filling.

So how do you listen completely? Well it's easy. Actually it's not, but it sounds easy (how appropriate). It does however require lots of practice. And we mean lots of practice. In fact, we're not finished practicing either. And we know of no one else who is either, or will ever be.

Here's what you do. Go into a conversation with the intention of only listening to fully understand what the other person is saying. Listen to them and hear them. Grasp it. Comprehend it. Stretch to make sense of it and to see it from their perspective. Work at it and then make sure you understand what they're saying by asking them if you understand it correctly. Re-state their perspective for them and have them give you the sign-off on whether or not you comprehend it.

Then, and only then, are you allowed to focus on what you want to say. Once you really understand what the other person is talking about, then you have two things going for you, 1) you can speak more effectively for them to understand you, since you can relate it to what they're saying, and 2) you can make sure that you're not saying the same thing in different ways. Once there was a meeting where two people began having a very animated discussion about some philosophical point. They were both convinced they were right, and were saying it very emphatically in order to convince the other person. Except they were both voicing the same opinion. Our friend Jeanne Chatigny summed it up by telling them both that she, "just witnessed a vehement agreement."

Want to start a great conversation? Start it by listening. Forget your perspective. Just listen. Turn your opinions off. Listen to understand. Never mind what you know is right. Defer judgment. Listen completely. And see where the conversation takes you. Be brave, you are about to enter the uncharted land of true synergy.

Seeking and Supporting Positive Deviants

We both belong to and are on the faculty of an organization called the Creative Education Foundation which sponsors the Creative Problem Solving Institute. Each June for the past 50 years or so, about a thousand creativity aficionados from around the world gather at the Institute for a week to improve their innovation skills and share what they've been learning about how to make creativity happen more easily and frequently. It is a VERY creative environment and culture (this is an understatement).

One of the core characteristics of the social atmosphere is a very high degree of tolerance for individuals who are outside of what would be called average or normal. That tolerance, acceptance, and even embracing attitude grows out of a long experience with the process of fostering creative organizations and communities.

Innovation Teams are constantly vigilant for "group-think," and seek the interaction of individuals who see things a little (or a lot) differently from everyone else. They go beyond just tolerance of individuals who are a little outside the norm to actively seeking them for inclusion on their team. If the individual meets the basic Innovation Team criteria of being an effective communicator, or desiring win-win solutions, and of having passion for the work of the team, then their different perspective will certainly forward the agenda of the team.

One day in 1943, Edwin Land and his 3-year old daughter, Jennifer, were spending an enjoyable afternoon around Santa Fe, NM, taking pictures. They had a great time, and shot many rolls of film. At the end of the day, when the young girl asked to see the pictures they had taken that day. Ed had to explain that the film had to be processed and printed and that it would take about a week. His daughter, not being an expert in the field of photography asked, "Why can't I see the pictures now?" An interesting question that Ed took to heart. So much so that after lots and lots of development and research, the Polaroid Land camera came into existence bringing nearly instant photos to the world. Ed's daughter played the role of the positive deviant on the Polaroid development team. And led to a multi-million dollar business.

Another example: in order to help a company resolve a problem on their production line, we put together a group, that included some people who were not experts in running the line. This did not set well with the line supervisor, because he wanted experts! He practically demanded people who really knew the machinery and could really contribute to the problem solving. We held our ground, and wore him down. Once everybody started generating ideas for how to solve the problem, one of the "non-experts" (we won't call him an idiot) began asking questions. Really dumb questions. The kind of questions that made the line supervisor roll his eyes…at first. Before he started to think. Which added to the richness of the ideas. As did the non-expert, who began suggesting some pretty wild and naïve ideas. Which really sparked some great ideas that, yes, solved the problem. Dumb questions? Yes. Stupid ideas? Right-O. Solved problem? Absolutely. Value of "ignorant" perspectives? Priceless.

Do you understand that we think diversity fuels innovation? We'll repeat it a lot. Sorry, but it needs repeating.

Like Attracts Like

World Wrestling Federation fans like to hang out with other World Wrestling federation fans. Republicans like being with other Republicans. People who have the same values and opinions like to be around those who validate and support those values. Innovative thinkers and doers like to hang out with other creative types. If you want to surround yourself with people who are working for SUCCESS, then live the values and lifestyle that you know are needed to create that. You'll attract others who hold the same interest. People who are great listeners attract great listeners. An individual who is skilled at deferring judgment will gradually find themselves in the company of others who defer judgment well. Individuals who are great teammates will find themselves on great teams.

But it takes time.

And you'll still have plenty of folks around you who are not living up to the standards we are presenting here. You can pout about that if you want. Poor you!

Or, you can buckle down and make the personal choice to be a great human being, regardless of what the world is doing around you. Exercise your ultimate freedom as a human being: to choose, at any given moment, how you are going to react to a given situation.

Here is the immutable law of social dynamics: You will gradually be surrounded with exactly what you put out to the world.. And we're not just talking about the trash people throw out their car window. As the Bible says, "you reap what you sow." Be a great parent, and you'll have other great parents around you. Care deeply about the welfare of others and you'll attract people who care deeply for you. The phrase "We create our own reality" sounds about as metaphysical as you could get, but it's the truth. Our reality is not what happens to us, but how we think and behave in the face of what happens to us.

Attracting the kind of people who help you grow your Innovation Team is up to you. We know you're going to do what's needed. Thanks.

In humans, like attracts like.

Listening to Your "Self Talk"

We talk to ourselves all the time. Some of us do it out loud, others through the dialogue in our head. But if you're having thoughts, you're doing it. Helloooo! Is anyone home?

Now here's the thing: you have the ability to decide what your thoughts are going to be about. To choose where you are going to place your attention. It's called free will. We just have to make the choice to exercise it. Doing so is a major component of creating what you want in your life and on your Innovation Team.

The challenge here is to pay attention to how you're thinking about the problems that you are struggling with at any given time. You see, we can make some accurate predictions about what your mind will do with certain types of thought forms:

Whenever you make a statement to yourself, your mind will search for evidence to support that statement.

Whenever you ask yourself a question, your mind will search for an answer.

Once you decide on an answer (essentially, make a statement to yourself that the answer is _____) your mind will look for evidence to support that answer and discard evidence which challenges it.

Once you place another person in a category (like "jerk") your mind will find evidence to strengthen the bars of the prison you have created for them. (And we can be mean, sadistic, stubborn, heartless jailers…of both others and ourselves.) There's a hacksaw on the next page…keep reading.

If you're not paying attention to the thoughts you're letting yourself have, you're going to get yourself in trouble.

Never say, "I can't do that." Rather, say "I can't do that yet." (Remember, there is a difference between what you won't do because of your values and what you can't do because of current limitations.)

Never say, "It's impossible." Rather, ask, "In what ways might it be possible?"

Never stop at the first answer. Rather, ask yourself if there might be other answers worth considering, and don't stop considering until you feel confident that you can clearly answer the question "Have I considered enough options?" with a centered "Yes."

There once was a monastery in which lived five Monks, the sole surviving members of a declining religious order. Each had dedicated their entire adult life to furthering the mission of the order and were deeply saddened by their inability to attract young novices so that their mission might out-live them. Living in the forest nearby was a very old retired Rabbi who had developed a large, prosperous, supportive and on-going community within and around his synagogue. As the Monks were discussing their dilemma at dinner one night, the idea arose of sending one of them to visit with the Rabbi and seek his wisdom. So a Monk was chosen, and left to visit their neighbor.

If you won't listen to yourself, then who will you listen to?

After some socializing and discussion of the problem which faced the Monks, the Rabbi, with evident sadness, asserted that he had no solution to the Monks' plight. So his visitor stood to take his leave. As he stepped through the door, the Rabbi said, "There is a curious thing though…in my dreams and prayer, I have been consistently getting the message that the Messiah is among you five."

The Monk returned to his colleagues with the sad truth that the Rabbi had no guidance, but also shared his cryptic comment about the presence of the Messiah among them.

Within a short time, the monastery was filled with novices, and the order was once again effectively carrying forward its mission.

What changed? The attention of the Monks was turned from "What a failure we have made of it." to "Which one of us might be the Messiah?" And through this question, evidence of the greatness in each of the Monks was found. They became attracted to that greatness in each other, and inspired by it to increase their own standard of behavior. Great people doing good works with and for each other attract other great people wishing to do great works with and for each other.

The only difference was where the Monks placed their attention.

So pay attention to all of the voices in your head and make

them live by the rules of a wise person. Ultimately, the only thing in your control is what you think. If you choose to be in control of what you think.

More on "Minding" One Another

Read the header carefully: this is not about "morons minding one another." That's when we talk each other into doing something real stupid. You remember, like that time when you were in high school and... Or when two or more people have joined in the game "ain't it awful..."

In the introduction to this chapter, we wrote about the powerful effect that allowing another's thoughts to suffuse your mind has on the quality of your relationship. We want to explore more deeply the connection this has to creativity.

We're talking synergy here with a capital "S". If you don't believe in magic, this stuff is going to challenge that belief when you get to feel it. Yes feel it. When we really connect previously unconnected thoughts while working individually or in a group, it is a real high. One of the best "natural highs" that we've ever experienced (and one of us has sought out and experienced most of them).

And there's only one way to get there: Listening.

Yes, getting high through listening.

Listening so deeply to another that you can experience the concept, problem, or situation fully from their perspective. Listening so deeply to the source of intuition that you are able to connect to stuff you've never connected to before. Don't worry, you won't loose yourself, (although it feels possible sometimes and we can be afraid of deep listening for that reason), you'll grow yourself. Become more. And if you've been reading along and are working at becoming more proficient at managing your thoughts, you're going to be better at listening, better at connecting, better at creating. All told, a great person to be around.

Will you risk it? Maybe we should look at the dynamics of risk for a bit. Coming right up!

NOTE TO INNOVATION TEAM MEMBERS:
If you want to get someone's attention, just listen.

Recap:

THE MOTTO: We need to listen to understand, then speak so we can be understood. Then we need to make sure everybody got it right!

The Subtle Truth About Active Listening - Active listening - really listening well - leads to great ideas and healthy relationships. The bottom line is that it requires someone to have the mental discipline and emotional maturity to shut up and listen…and just listen. And somebody has to go first. Will it be you?

A Word About Body Language - You can either spend time working on manipulating your body language to let people know what you think, or you can spend time managing your thoughts so that your body expresses what you really are thinking. The latter is the more effective approach to genuine communication.

The Art of Apology - Just saying, "I'm sorry," isn't enough. You have to really understand from the other person's perspective what you did that was wrong and how it made them feel. And you need to feel bad. Once you feel bad and understand it and communicate it, then you can say, "I'm sorry." As long as it's genuine. And as long as you can commit to some action to ensure it will never happen again. Now that's artful apology!

The use of Intuition - Intuition is knowing something accurately without consciously understanding why you know it. Innovation team members take data from anywhere they can get it. Intuition is one of those places. So listen to your intuition. It's trying to tell you something…insightful.

Incubation: The Value of Doing Nothing - Stuck on a problem? Walk away. Great ideas come at strange times when the brain is working on auto-pilot doing something else. So let your brain think while you're taking a walk or doing something you enjoy or stepping away from the desk. And be ready to record the great ideas!

The Value of the Gut Check - Logic be damned. We're really driven by our "gut." By our intuition and internal programming. By our beliefs and attitudes. Not by what necessarily makes sense objectively. The more important the decision, the less we use rational criteria. So be aware of your "gut," honor it, respect it, treat it to the occasional chocolate chip cookie (that was my gut talking), and you'll consciously make smarter decisions. And yes, we'll share the cookie.

Style Differences in Team Members - People are different. Everybody has different styles. Instead of trying to find team members with the same styles, embrace the differences, and let the friction spark great ideas.

Creating Different Perspectives on The Team - There is nothing more damaging than "group-think," so make sure you have diverse perspectives when you're working on something. In fact, you may want to appoint an "agent provocateur" to generate valuable conflicting opinions.

Phrase Problems as Questions to Put Problems in Jeopardy - Want to break through your problem? Then stop stating it as an obstacle. Phrase it as a question, which naturally invites your brain to offer up solutions. Start them with:

> How to
> How might
> In what ways might
> What might be all the

The Power of the Agenda - For the most effective team meetings, have an overt agenda of what's going to happen. Include: 1) purpose, 2) process, 3) outcome, and 4) timing.

Listening Completely - It sounds simple, but it takes a couple of lifetimes to perfect it. Here's what you do. Listen. Just listen. Listen to them and hear them. Grasp it. Comprehend it. Stretch to make sense of it and to see it from their perspective. Work at it and then make sure you understand what they're saying by asking them if you understand it correctly. Re-state their perspective for them and have them confirm whether or not you comprehend it.

Seeking and Supporting Positive Deviants - Seek people on the team with different perspectives who can help the team by asking "dumb" questions that will spark smart answers.

Like Attracts Like - Since like attracts like, if you want to be with great people, be great. Want a great team? Be a great team member. Want to work with creative people? Show them how it's done. Gandhi said it this way, "You must first be the change you wish to see in the world."

Listening to Your "Self Talk" - Your brain seeks evidence of all of the conclusions and categories that you create. So you can alter your perspective of the world by managing how you talk to your self about you, others, and everything. Choose to see other people as great, and your brain will start listing all the things they do that are great. Choose to see yourself as a great team member, and yup, there it is, a list of reasons why you are. Is it really that simple? Yup, simple...yet difficult to do. Start practicing now.

Morons...oops...More On Minding One Another - Listen, listen, listen. Just listen. If you can do that, then we're not just morons waiting for our turn to speak and impress, we're being great Innovation Team members who are working at understanding their team-mates. And through understanding emerges Innovation. Isn't that what you asked for?

A POEM ON LISTENING...

When I ask you to listen to me and you start giving advice, you have not done what I asked. When I ask you to listen to me and you begin to tell me why I shouldn't feel that way, you are trampling on my feelings. When I ask you to listen to me and you feel you have to do something to solve my problem, you have failed me, strange as that may seem.

All I asked was that you listen, not talk or do - just listen to me.

Advice is cheap: 50 cents will get you both Dear Abby and Billy Graham in the same newspaper. And I can do for myself: I'm not ehlpless, maybe discouraged and faltering, but not helpless.

When you do something for me that I can and need to do for myself, you contribute to my fear and weakness.

But when you accept as a simple fact that I do feel what I feel, no matter how irrational, then I can quit trying to convince you and can get about the business of understanding what is behind this irrational feeling. And when that is clear, the answers are obvious and I don't need advice. Irrational feelings make sense when we understand what is behing them.

Perhaps that is why prayer works, sometimes, for some people, because God is mute and He doesn't give advice or try to fix things. He just listens and lets you work it out for yourself.

So, please listen and just hear me. And, if you want to talk, wait a minute for your turn; and I'll listen to you.

--Author unknown (but we wish we knew, can you help?)

4

Cultivate Risk Taking

*"Cautious, careful people, always casting about to preserve their reputations...
can never effect a reform."*

-- Susan B. Anthony

Innovation thrives in an environment where calculated risk is the rule. We're not talking foolish impetuousness here, but neither are we talking about not always holding mommy and daddy's hands. We have to put ourselves in a place where failure is a possibility. If we don't, we stay stuck. We can't be growing-ups. We can't be great members of the team. We can't contribute to innovation.

Now here's what doesn't work: "I'll take a risk with you once I feel safe." Duh. You'll never feel safe with me until you take a risk and find out that I treat you well. In this case it's clear: the chicken goes last. Sure, sometimes you'll get burned. You'll also get over it. That's what growing-ups do.

We wish we could tell you that a life on an Innovation Team is all roses and rainbows. It's not. There will be pain. But if you and your teammates have surrendered to your humanity, the pain will be less intense and less long lasting. We know of one manager in the toy industry who actually threw a party to celebrate an expensive failure caused by an oversight in the design of a toy created by one of his Innovation Teams. As related to us by one of the team members (with glowing admiration), the team leader said, "I'm constantly pushing you to come up with innovative toy concepts…I know that this is going to mean an occasional failure. I know you all hate the failure probably more than I do. I want to celebrate that we are pushing the envelope."

It's as if we have risk muscles that, if exercised, become easier to use. So pushing yourself to take risk in one arena of your life will make it easier to take risk in another. Taking a chance on an honest, revealing comment with a friend makes it easier to float an "out of bounds" idea in your work group. Admitting a failure at work makes it easier to apologize at home. Cultivate a life of risk- taking.

By the way, we're talking about emotional risk here though, not physical risk. It seems that taking physical risks doesn't necessarily translate into increased ability to take emotional risk. We saw that a lot in our early years of team-building when we were using adventure-based activities like rock climbing and whitewater rafting as team-building techniques. It created a lot of "rah rah" and esprit de corps, but no real increase in innovation.

So quit wimping out. Open up your heart. Open up your mind. Open up your life. Innovation in teams demands it.

The Value of Failure

The Setting: Merchant Marine ships in and around England being sunk by German U-boats in the early days of World War II.

The Players: Young, fit sailors. Old crusty out-of-shape sailors.

Scene One: Boat sinks, all sailors in the water.

Scene Two: Young, fit sailors drowning.

Scene Three: Old crusty out-of-shape sailors being rescued.

Analysis: The young guys, having survived fewer adversities in their lives, gave up quicker. The old guys, having survived more, had just that much more "stick-to-itiveness"

So, Kurt Hahn, an educator, created a program to expose the younger sailors to intense emotional and physical challenges (yes, both) that were picked for their ability to be perceived initially as insurmountable. Yet if the individuals called fully on their own resources and those of the group, the challenges could be overcome. The result: the survival rate for young sailors on torpedoed ships increased significantly. That program survives to this day, and is known worldwide as Outward Bound.

The "stick to it and survive" instinct is honed through overcoming difficult challenges that involve many small failures along the way. The only way to have the perseverance needed to handle the really big challenges is to be willing to take the risk to throw yourself at the small ones and to weather failures in the process of surmounting them. The only way to develop the people on an Innovation Team is to reward risk-taking, not just success. The only way to learn to discern which risks are too big, too likely to lead to failure, or just insurmountable at this time with the current resources, is to have failed in that discernment in the past. When you never fail, you're not really learning where the edge is. And today, any company that is not right on the edge is going to be left behind. In the dust. Playing catch-up. Loosing share. Getting bought at a discount.

When we were novice rock climbers, we judged our degree of pushing ourselves by whether we were falling or not. We knew that when we went through periods of not falling, it wasn't because we were great climbers, it was because we weren't pushing ourselves to our personal edge.

Likewise, when learning how to sail small boats quickly for racing, the old adage holds: "If you're not tipping over sometimes, you're not learning."

Ernest Hemingway said, "Life breaks everyone. However, some people end up stronger in the broken places." We'll show you our scars if you'll show us yours…

Hopefully, you've failed more than once in your life-to-date. And hopefully, you picked yourself up, brushed off the dust and came at the problem from a different perspective…

Or -- now here's the heretical notion -- walked away. Yup, walked away. Hopped on the bus Gus, made a new plan Stan, tried not to be coy Roy, just listen to me*. This is the place of killing a momentum-filled project when, because the environment has changed, it's no longer a good idea. It's backing off of Mt. Everest when the weather turns bad. It's realizing that the best way to deal with diversity is not segregation. Getting out of silicone breast implants once the evidence is clear about their danger. Reversing the "New Coke" juggernaut. Taking money away from DARE programs and putting it someplace effective (Five independent studies have demonstrated DARE's lack of effect).

Backing off the summit requires the willingness and maturity of the team members to speak up with an idea that is counter to the momentum of the group. It can be a very unpopular place to be. Team members may think you're a party-pooper, a spoil-sport, or a heretic. We experience this when we make such public statements about something very popular like DARE. But talk is cheap. We're trying to practice what we preach.

Failure can be great. If we recognize it, take our lumps, pick ourselves up, and start a new game. Having learned from the failure.

*With apologies to Paul and/or Art.

Risk, and the Stupid Idea

We see this all of the time when we're teaching groups to be more creative. When generating ideas to overcome a problem, it's really hard to let yourself go and defer judgment like a crazy person. Like you're out of your mind. Like you don't really care.

But it's precisely that kind of attitude that yields innovation in divergent thinking. And it requires risk. You have to be willing to say the thing that you know is stupid. It popped into your mind for a reason. Contribute it to the divergence.

But we want you to go even further. (Pushy, aren't we?) We want you to take the risk to look for the stupid ideas and contribute them to the thinking of the group. To actually give yourself the challenge of reaching a notable mistake quotient. Why? You know that answer by now: the effectiveness of the creative process is directly proportional to the ability to defer judgment. You're not really diverging effectively unless you are willing to take the risk to say the thing that you are judging already.

Yes, it's easier to do if you trust the people you're with, but remember: trust comes after risk taking, not before it. And since you're the leader of the Innovation Team, and 67% of the team's creative behavior is dependent on the creativebehavior of the leader, you've just gotta do it. It's up to you to go first.

So whattaya waiting for? You've never asked anyone's permission to be stupid before. Go for it! Do it by choice rather than by accident.

The mark of real genius is understanding that stupidity is a choice at the right time, not an accident over which you have no control.

Seeking Reckless (Wreckless) Solutions: Big Risk, Big Payoffs

Can recklessness lead to less wrecks? Yes.

(By the way, we know our English teacher said it's "fewer wrecks," but that doesn't sound as snappy does it? Our apologies to all

English teachers reading this, especially Ms. Nina Wright.)

We all know that big payoffs come from big risks. Those stories are legendary, especially in the culture of the United States. We're a nation that values taking risks. Stories like 1) Columbus convincing Queen Isabella to let him search for a trade route to India by sailing west, 2) the pioneers settling North America, 3) Edison and the light bulb, 4) Steven Jobs and the Macintosh personal computer, 5) Debbie Fields and Mrs. Fields' Cookies, 6) Amazon.com (although the jury's still out), 7) Bill Gates and the first personal computer operating system, or 8) having children (although in our case, the jury's still out). Clearly, all of these examples require great risk of different varieties: personal, financial, emotional, security, or reputation.

And the payoffs are tremendous. Life would be very different were it not for the risks of these pioneers. And in some cases, it would be unlivable. Especially in the case of Mrs. Fields (okay, we're cookieholics, we admit it), who was told by "the experts" that consumers preferred crispy over soft, chewy cookies (see "The Value of the Gut Check" in the chapter "Conscious Listening, Clear Speaking").

So, deep in our consciousness, we know that risk is critical for success, especially big, earth-shaking, world-changing, fabulous-riches-creating success. But wow, is it difficult and rare. Especially because of all of them. You know who they are: your boss, your spouse, your peers, your banker, your lawyer, your children, your parents, your friends, your enemies, or your hair-stylist (the source of all true wisdom). Oh…and don't forget your………self.

In spite of the fact that we know risk is important, we have a tendency to shy away, because we don't want to be seen making mistakes. We don't want to have failure on our "permanent record." We don't want to be associated with a flop.

How unfortunate.

Thomas Edison failed over 3,000 times to develop a working prototype of a light bulb before he succeeded. Imagine failing day after day after day. Trying one different type of filament after another. Letting all of his employees see the failure of his idea over and over and over again. He must have developed a

real complex, right? Nope, not old Thomas. After the first
thousand mistakes, he said, "Well, we're making progress -- we
know a thousand ways it can't be done. We're that much closer
to getting there." Stubborn old goat.

And he went through this again later in his career, after 5000
attempts, he invented an electrical storage battery. Like
the Energizer® Bunny, he just kept trying, and trying,
and trying...

What an inspiration! Tom Peters (the management consult-
ant guru) identifies three keys to business success: 1) test fast,
2) fail fast, 3) adjust fast. Yes, fail fast. Find the holes. Ready?
Fire! Aim. Find where it doesn't work. Find the flops. Because they're there. And if they're not, then you're playing too
safe. You're not taking the big leaps that yield greatness.

Too bad.

Mistakes are critical for success. If you can find the little mistakes as you move along, you are less likely to make The Big
Mistake at the end. Finding the failures early on reduces the
likelihood of the Big Flop. The Failed Product. The Unsuccessful Strategy. The Bad Investment. The Botched Relationship. The Unsuccessful Line.

So early recklessness, when identified and fixed, can yield results that aren't wrecks, but are in fact successes. Identifying
light bulbs that don't work will get you that much closer to big
ideas that do work.

Remember, Babe Ruth, the baseball great who is remembered
as the Home Run King? Mr. Ruth held the home run record
for years and years, but what most of us forget is that he also
had a record number of strikeouts. The Babe stated his philosophy this way, "Never let the fear of striking out get in your
way."

That's a winning attitude.

Especially when you're taking another piece of Edison's advice, "There is always a better way. Find it." It will be worth it.
Want proof? Remember, if Edison hadn't believed that, you'd
be reading this by the light of a kerosene lamp and we'd be
writing this on our laptop computers by candlelight.

The "Heretical Notion:" Voicing &Killing "Sacred Cows"

(Again, with apologies to our friends at PETA)

The most effective way to create some powerful innovation with your team is to be the "heretic." To identify the most important concept of the project, strategy, organization or group. And then mark it as "wrong," and worthy of changing.

Then sit back and listen to the uproar.

When it's died down, see if you can't find some real value in the new perspective. We call this the "heretical notion." It's the opinion of the heretic, the rebel. It's also known as "killing the (metaphorical) sacred cows.*" Or as our friend Jerry Hirshberg calls it (in his book "The Creative Priority"), "Embracing the dragon."

It's amazing how stuck and habitualized and routinized we can get in our thinking. We've seen it and heard it in ourselves and others. It sounds like this, "we can only do it this way..." or "this is the way we've always done it..." or "it only works when you do this."

When you see such behavior or hear these phrases, your ears should perk up. You should put on your heretic uniform, get out your axe, and prepare to embrace the dragon. This is the time to voice the "heretical notion" and try to spark some real change. It's the moment of potential paradigm change, and can yield some huge results.

George Bernard Shaw said it this way, "All great truths begin as blasphemies." Examples:

"Everyone knows the world is flat."

"Heavier than air flying machines are impossible."

"Humankind will never walk on the moon."

"There is a market for about five computers in the world."

"The concept of reliable overnight delivery service is not feasible."

These are some well-known (metaphorical) sacred cows that have since been digested as (figurative) hamburger. How many more exist for you and your Innovation Team? Thousands. Millions. Bazillions! It hurts to think about how many of them there are. They're just hard to find because they're so ingrained in you and us and the culture. We're always looking for them and yet we're still surprised when we find them. Right in front of our noses.

How embarrassing. Yet how rewarding!

*No animals were injured or killed in the writing of this chapter. Nor do we advocate killing any animals. But feel free to kill habitual thinking that gets in the way of real progress.

Risk-taking and Environments that Foster Innovation

Time to go back to the research. Please get out your academic regalia and bear with us.

There are two organizational climate assessments (surveys) that we respect that do a great job of determining the climate of organization with respect to Innovation (The KEYS Assessment and the Situational Outlook Questionnaire). In other words; they identify the characteristics of an organization that help or hinder innovation and creativity.

A common element of both assessments is the inclusion of risk-taking as an essential component of an innovative organization or team. So you don't have to take our word for it, trust the researchers on this one.

Of course risk-taking looks different in various types of organizations. We know of one organization, for example, where a very low measure for "risk-taking" was deemed very appropriate. The organization made explosives. Yet we've worked with heavily regulated industries (like banking and radioactive pharmaceuticals) where certain types of risks are definitely illegal or deadly. Stay away from those types of risks. However, try doing some things differently within the rules. That's the risk-zone. We do not advocate taking risks that will get you fired, killed, or worse.

So risk carefully, and risk where appropriate. Take some risks in terms of trusting people you have to work with but don't know. Risk suggesting some silly ideas. Risk trying something that's new and different (but not dangerous!). Risk your reputation for success through honesty. Risk trying a new place for lunch. Then prepare to be amazed, but don't be disappointed if it doesn't pay off. Learn from it. After all, the research says that we learn more from our mistakes than our successes. Then celebrate your willingness to push your personal envelope, like the manager from the Toy Company.

Congratulations! You risked! You failed! You learned! What a great day. Now flip your tassel.

Creating Passion Through Polarity: The Productive Tension of Opposite Viewpoints

What creates risk? Often it's fear. The fear of conflict and rejection. The fear of saying something that another person won't like or will think is wrong, bad, different, stupid, naive, out-of-bounds, or wacky. Or the fear of being proved wrong, bad, different, etc. The safe bet? Say nothing. Play it safe. Don't rock the boat. Go with the prevailing opinion. Agree with everyone. Sounds like a friendly team, right?

Maybe. But it also sounds like a recipe for a stultifying lack of innovation. Yawn. And we really don't need any more recipes for that, now do we?

So what can we do to create some new perspectives? We've talked about being a contrarian...not a "devil's advocate" (usually code for people looking for an excuse to decimate a new idea - "let me play devil's advocate and tell you why your idea stinks..."), but creating new perspectives. Bucking the trends. Looking for new insights. Looking for alternative conclusions. Good contrarians actually are able to toss perspectives into the mix that they don't personally believe in. It's like the debate team mentality. Being personally able to argue both sides of a point, irrespective of what you actually believe. A good contrarian makes sure that opposite viewpoints are considered just long enough to be sure that all of the merits of that viewpoint have the opportunity to be incorporated into the way the team is moving forward. Then she/he lets go.

Want a systems approach to help you create that? Well we mentioned how Jerry Hirshberg, president of Nissan Design International, hires automotive designers in pairs. These pairs are completely opposite in their viewpoints and the way they do things. We'd take it a step further and tie their compensation together so that neither one of them benefits unless they both work together effectively. They could consider themselves "married" forever. "You grow, I grow. You go, I go.

This way they have the incentive to use their different viewpoints productively. In order to both succeed together, they must see how to make newness out of differentness.

Does this create conflict? Sometimes, yes. At least until the opposite pairs figure out how to team together.

Karen Strickholm of the Strickholm Company handled it this way. She had two employees who were supposed to work together, yet who weren't getting along. They were arguing, fighting, blaming the other when things went wrong...you know the signals. She sent them out to lunch and told them not to come back until they had figured it out and could get along. The threat if they couldn't figure it out and work together productively? They'd both be fired.

It worked.

We're each different. Deal with it and thrive.

It's not enough just to have different perspectives, it's important to put those together to create the innovation. Look at it this way: it's about forcing together two unrelated things in order to create a new idea. How do you create water and fire in order to make something productive? Use it to create steam to power an engine. How do you make oil and water work together? You use their natural repulsion to each other to make the printing process of lithography work. How do you make your perspective of black work with their opinion of white? Look for some new shades of gray. Or some very exciting checkerboard patterns. You know the old expression; "opposites attract?" Well what they attract are exciting new perspectives.

So look for where the diverse perspectives can fit together. Look for how the differences can be exploited. Dream up some unusual combinations. Figure out how it can be one thing and also another at the same time. Create some new alloys out of divergence and see how they fit together.

Remember, stainless steel was an experimental alloy that didn't do what it was supposed to, so it was thrown on the scrap heap. Where someone eventually noticed that it didn't rust. Hence, a new material with millions of uses. All from combining some new materials and not being satisfied with leaving the resultant product on the scrap heap.

The Myth of the One Right Answer

Two and two equals four, right? Of course. Is it the only right answer? Well, if we believe what we learned in Miss Meinke's first grade class, then the answer is, "yes." Or else you received a big red check mark, indicating "one wrong." One wrong answer.

Except that sometimes two and two equals twenty-two. Sometimes it's two squared (okay, still four, but from a different perspective). Sometimes it's zero (if there's a minus sign between them). Sometimes, as a mathematical scholar will tell you, it's 10 (in base three). Or 20 (in base two). Sometimes it's a short dress worn by a ballet dancer (a tutu). It's a leader in South Africa, a group for playing bridge, a piece of lumber, a quad, a quad track, and an educational concept at a college offering an associates degree after two years and a bachelors degree after two more. Sometimes it's a golf ball about to land on your noggin (fore!!!).

But we digress. For (there we go again) innovation to happen in teams, there must be recognition that there is more than one right answer. Always. The culture of the team must embrace the fact that one answer is never enough. At least before a final decision has been made. Searching for lots of ideas and looking for multiple solutions is critical to innovation. Why?

Our colleague Roger Firestien, of the Center for Studies in Creativity, notes that if you set out to generate 30 ideas, the first third that you generate are the expected, usual, and banal answers (been there, seen that). The second third are wild, strange, and bizarre (yikes!). But the last third are the unusual and sophisticated ideas that yield some real innovation (aha!). And that's what we want to cultivate.

If you and the group can't turn off the gator brain and get past the notion that you have to find the one right answer, you'll never find some of the more novel, simple, elegant, or slick answers that can change the world. Edison said it, "there is always a better way. Find it."

Does the tungsten filament incandescent light bulb work? Sure. So does the fluorescent bulb. And the mercury lamp. And the halogen bulb. And the Light Emitting Diode (LED). And the high-discharge xenon bulb. And are they all great answers for their applications? Absolutely.

Never stop finding right ideas, and you'll always get better. And isn't that the goal?

Do Something Every Day that Scares You

So how does one cultivate risk? We'll give you a hint: look at the section headline (above).

Now before you break out in a cold sweat at the thought of skiing the Himalayas or bungee-jumping off of the Empire State Building, hang on. We're talking about very small emotional risks. Which for everyone will be different. For some people, that may be saying hello to the toll taker and giving them a big smile. For others, it may be wearing plaid pants. For someone else, it might be asking for a raise, trying a new kind of food, or asking a stranger for directions. Understand that we're not asking you to run naked in traffic. In fact, we're actively dissuading you from running naked in traffic. Really. It's just not safe. Unless you have some SPF 45 sunscreen. And even then...

We're talking about small steps here. We're talking about stretching your comfort zone a little bit at a time, which leads, over time, to a much wider, bigger, fatter comfort zone. It's like creating an ocean one drop at a time. The first few...several...million drops won't create the next Atlantic, but eventually those drops add up.

So it is with risk. By doing one small thing each day, you make it easier and easier to take risks. Not physical risks, but emotional risks.

And emotional risks are the things that will lead to you being a better member of an Innovation Team, and a more creative person in general. And that is the point right? Or is this book supposed to be about knitting pretty potholders (which for either of us would be a risk to take tomorrow)?

So put this on your daily list of things to do: "Take a risk." Put it in your day-planner, on your "To Do" list, your personal digital assistant, on a Post-it note in your work space, or write it on the palm of your hand. More important though, is to just do it (with apologies - and thanks - to Nike®).

Want some ideas of risks to take every day? Here's a brief divergent list to help you out:

How to take a risk today

Eat at a new restaurant.

Call that friend that you've been meaning to call.

Accept the challenge of making a surly cashier smile.

Challenge yourself to be the waitress's favorite customer. And let them know it.

Tell somebody that you love, that you love them.

Wear plaid pants.

Sit down with a close co-worker or boss, and sincerely ask them for feedback (what they like and what areas for improvement you have).

Ask for a raise.

Schedule time with your boss and ask how you can help them advance so that you can get their job.

Take a different route to work.

Sing in public, either in a Karaoke bar or elsewhere.

Whistle tunes as you walk through a grocery store.

Wear fancy underwear.

Wave to everyone you drive past.

Pay the toll for the car behind you.

Pay the toll for the car two cars behind you, but tell the toll person to tell the benefactor that it was the car in front of them (think through the dynamics of that). (Thanks to our friend Bill Frost).

Speak gibberish (or a foreign language) at the checkout counter, and only use pantomime to express your need.

Get your face painted.

Wear your shoes backwards until someone notices.

Shave (or don't shave) your facial hair.

Tell two people today that you appreciate them, and why.

Give money to a panhandler.

Volunteer for a committee.

Anonymously pay for someone's dinner in a restaurant.

Buy the entire restaurant a round of Jell-O (with thanks to Penn & Teller).

Bake cookies for co-workers.

Get in the car & start driving, to an unknown destination.

Go and introduce yourself to neighbors.

Pick up trash on the street.

Give a tip at the drive through window.

Call the tobacconist and ask if they have "Prince Albert in a Can."

Write a letter to the editor.

Clean up an empty lot.

Send a blank check to Jonathan and Bob.

Send two blank checks to us!

Sit in the front row at church, or anywhere else.

Join Toastmasters.

Go see one of "those" movies, the kind that you never go see.

Pick up a magazine that you'd never ordinarily read.

Order a different kind of drink than you usually do.

Dance in your living room.

Go dancing.

Leave a really large tip at a restaurant.

Sit in a different chair in the meeting room.

Get a massage.

Switch the order of your morning routine in the bathroom.

Buy a new toothpaste.

Change your hair color.

Part your hair on the other side.

Get contact lenses OR wear your glasses to work.

Ask your teenager for their fashion opinion.

Listen to different kind of music.

Listen to your teenager's kind of music.

Get tinted contacts.

Compliment a stranger.

Give flowers to a stranger and tell them they're from someone else who swore you to secrecy.

Eat an exotic food.

Rearrange your office furniture.

Take dancing lessons.

Trade sides of the desk with your office visitors.

Try a new piece of equipment at the gym.

Upgrade your computer software (No way! That's beyond the bounds of common sense!).

Strike up a conversation at the gym.

When a waiter asks you if you'd like anything else, ask for world peace and a new Ferrari.

Build a Lego structure on your desk during your lunch hour.

Face the "wrong" wall when you're in the elevator.

Take a date to a Disney movie.

Without warning, give your date/spouse a "raspberry" on their neck.

Bring your child to work on a day when it's not expected.

Have chair races down the hall.

Throw a Frisbee during lunch.

Invite your colleagues over for dinner.

Eat lunch at Chuck E. Cheez.

Wear white pants before Memorial Day (wearing "winter white" is cheating).

Say hello to strangers.

Write a list of things you can do in order to do something everyday that scares you.

So pick one. Just one, and do it today. Do it right now. Do it before you do anything else. C'mon! Take the Risk. JUST DO IT!

Oh, and the last one for the list above: buy a new pair of sneakers. (Gee, I wonder wear that one came from?)

Recap:

THE MOTTO: I learn only when I'm willing to make mistakes. Today I want to learn a lot, so I'm expecting lots of mistakes!

The Value of Failure - Yeah, we hate it too, but we learn more from our failures…perhaps only from our failures! So if you're not putting something on the line (we don't advocate risking life, limb and family) and losing occasionally, you're not learning much and you're not on the path to greatness. Unless you're sometimes losing big, you're not winning big or growing.

Risk and the Stupid Idea - High-level innovation requires everyone to submit really stupid ideas. Not because stupid ideas are (necessarily) creative, but because it's what creates the atmosphere of creativity that's necessary for innovative new ideas. An atmosphere that says, "we're open to odd, funny looking ideas, so pitch it to us!" And even if the ideas aren't big winners…at least they'll be fun!

Seeking Reckless (Wreckless) Solutions: Big Risk, Big Payoffs - Small risks (usually) yield small payoffs. So in order to create REAL innovation, it's necessary to fail many times before succeeding. This, then, is the value of failure. Short term failure yields long term success. Test fast, fail fast, adjust fast, in order to wreck less often.

The "Heretical Notion:" Voicing and Killing "Sacred Cows" - You know what they say about never assuming because it makes an "ass" of "u" and "me" (ass-u-me, get it?). The best way to smash assumptions is to find them and figure out ways around them. Especially when it seems like heresy, since that's usually the clue that you're about to create real innovation. Want killer ideas? Start challenging the status quo.

Risk-Taking and Environments that Foster Innovation - Risk creates innovation? Right. But don't just take our word for it since, according to solid research on innovative organizational climates, it's really true! So take an appropriate risk, and let the innovation begin.

Creating Passion Through Polarity: The Productive Tension of Opposite Viewpoints - Agreement is safe and pleasant. Contrary opinions are dicey, debate-starting, and sometimes contentious. They also create some amazingly great new ideas that people are passionate about! So stop surrounding yourself with people just like you and seek some other - different -- perspectives and opinions.

The Myth of the One Right Answer - One answer is only one answer. How profound. Yet in life (unlike 1st grade) there is almost always more than one correct answer. For innovative new ideas, generate as many of them as you can, and don't stop until you've got at least 30 or 50 or 200 or... As Alex Osborn once said, "quantity yields quality." The more answers you've got, the more likely you are to find more right ones, and more GREAT ones!

Do Something Everyday that Scares You - Emotional risks are required to stretch your comfort zone. A stretched comfort zone is necessary for breaking down the barriers that get in the way of being a great team member and creating innovation. So stretch the emotional barriers a little bit every day. Painful? Maybe. Valuable? More like, priceless!

5

Expect Win-Win

"Before a vision can become a reality, it must be owned by every single member of the group."

-- Phil Jackson (LA Lakers coach and former Chicago Bulls coach), author of *Sacred Hoops*

Win-Win, Win-Lose, Lose-Win, Lose-Lose. You know the drill.

Here's the only real option for Innovation Teams: It's gotta be Win-Win or no deal. But how?

You get there by taking the risk to listen well enough to another's ideas that you are able to come up with a way to create only good outcomes for everyone involved. We're talking about innovative synergy.

The problem is that a big chunk of our brainspace is dedicated to making sure that we win and they loose. It's about domination, hierarchy and survival in the swamp. You gotta get yours before they get theirs 'cause there ain't enough to go around. And kiddo, this is one tough dynamic for us to overcome. It takes a lot of maturity and innovative resource to stay win-win all of the time.

So much, in fact, that you'll probably never do it all of the time. But you can create a lot of innovation (not to mention a good deal of maturity) by trying.

The trick is to maintain vigilance for those reptilian brain behaviors that get in the way of partnering effectively with other people. And you must have an attitude of humility that allows for that vigilance. Pretty much as soon as you start to think you've got this Win-Win habit won, your conceit sets you up for yet another lesson in humility. But if you maintain the vigilance (and your innovative teammates are doing the same thing) you can catch the gator-brain before it bites a big chunk out of the innovation energy of the group.

It's not a matter of if you backslide into unproductive "lose" behaviors, it's a matter of when, and what form it will take. Another task made easier by lesson number one: Surrender to your humanity (but always strive to be more)!

Territoriality and the Reptilian Brain

Time for a trip to the swamp. Bring some bug repellent, a snack, and some waders. We're going to be there for a while.

As we've said before, innovation teams stay vigilant for the dynamics that their gator brains create in their interpersonal behaviors. But there's more to it when you layer on the more human dynamic of the need to exist in a social group. A family of gators, if you will. We're talking about the pecking order, but the reality that gets hidden behind the "bird" analogy is that we do a lot more than "peck" at each other. We can, will, and do take big bites. Gobble up. Kill.

It's not a nice truth about our nature, but to deny its existence is to court disaster. A frenetic feeding frenzy where it's every gator for itself. A wild, bloody, painful mess that stirs up even more muck from the bottom of the swamp. Old hurts. Past pains. Childhood "stuff." Family of origin dynamics. Complexity beyond the ability of any innovation doctor to fully heal.

So let's look at how hierarchy can play itself out in ways that work against being a great innovation team.

Option 1: *I'm a bigger gator than you are: I have to protect my position, and keep you in your place. I've got to be careful to not be vulnerable in front of you. I can't make mistakes. I need to point out your mistakes or praise your successes in such a way that I make it clear that success is the exception for you. The ultimate decisions must have my buy in, even if my opinion is in a minority group of one. You'll experience me as incredibly arrogant and closed to any idea I didn't think of.*

Option 2: *You're a bigger gator than I am: I need to defer to your opinion. I won't generate anything new until I run it throught the mental filter of how I think you'll react. I'm pre-disposed to overvalue your ideas, and undervalue mine. When someone else challenges you, and I agree with them, I duck-and-cover so that I'm not part of the collateral damage. I say "yes" when I want to say "no." You'll like me because I always seem to agree with you.*

Option 3: *We're both bigger gators than the rest of 'em: We maintain our bond, which may be an uneasy truce, by frequently reminding each other of our superiority over our swampmates. I'm watching your back, and you're watching mine. Yet I wonder what you say behind my back because I know what you say behind the back of others, and it's not nice. We're both victims of rapport building "on the cheap," and while there is a modicum of safety in numbers, we still feel vulnerable in our* *position. We have to hold the others down, but we worry that the other is throwing the extra food to a favorite who might rise to challenge our position as one of the two top gators. I like having you around, but at least part of the reason is that I don't like having you out of my sight.*

The Productive Option: *In innovation teams, hierarchy exists, but is task-dependent and constantly flexing. the decision of the team about who's the best gator in a given situation changes with the situation. There is no sense of permanence in any momentarily apparent hierarchy. Because each of us receives the same value from the success of all of us, we make decisions based on the needs of the challenge we are facing, rather than the need to maintain our safety by being dominant or submissive in the group. the only things that get gobbled up in an innovation team are metaphorical sacred cows, and we all agree, they're yummy! (Bonus! Since they're metaphors, they're non-fattening.)*

Growing and Developing Others

The way win/win really plays out beautifully on an Innovation Team is when the members are working to aid in the advancement of all the other members. You'll hear them saying great things about each other both inside and outside of the team. There is such a strong trust and concern for the people in the group that teammates see the advancement of one of their members as good for their own career as well. It's always good to have someone who knows and values you at the next level up in the organizational hierarchy.

Hard to come by, this concern for the others? Absolutely, captain! But if a critical mass of your teammates are walking the "win/win" walk, then you're going to see just such a degree of unselfish care emerge. You can increase its likelihood by consciously focusing on having a desire for growth for the others.

And if you really hold that value, you're going to be willing to share your insights with others on the team about what they might be doing to develop themselves. In an atmosphere of nonjudgmental, kindergartners-with-finger-paint, you'll all share a curiosity about learning, improving, and finding out just what you are capable of doing. And because you're debunking the myth of the grown-up more and more each day within the team, you're not afraid to offer suggestions, and you're not defensive when you hear them.

Cool! Work becomes about more than making money. It becomes about developing ourselves as human beings. And the bottom line of all of our lives is that we rarely lay on our deathbeds wishing we had made more dollars…too often it's that we had made more of ourselves. Here's the ride. You've got a pre-paid ticket. Hop on! You're about to have the time of your life. Screaming with your hands in the air is optional.

Establishing Group Norms

To get to the places we're talking about, you're going to need to have enough of your group pulling in the same way and choosing to act congruently with what it takes to have an Innovation Team. Achieving this kind of win/win culture is so difficult for us as human beings that anything less than a full-scale effort to make the shift is likely to fail. Developing an Innovation Team is difficult through "the gradual method." Jump in! What we're talking about here is fundamental connection to a new value system for working together.

History tells us that whenever a culture has been successful at gluing a new and improved value system to the psyches of the members of that culture, it has been accomplished through a process most commonly seen as a Rite of Passage.

In organizational development terms, it's a significant off-site training event.

Our experience is that there are two areas that a potential Innovation Team must focus on at the point of its inception if it is to function effectively, and that these new thinking and behavioral standards must be learned, discussed and practiced immediately, all at once, and in a concentrated form. The skills we are talking about here are so interwoven that it is almost impossible to do one well without focusing on the others at the same time.

The two areas are:

1) Attitudes, which fuel interpersonal behavior norms, and

2) Innovation tools and techniques, which fuel the group's efficiency. We discuss both extensively throughout these pages. Now, let's talk about how to get them to stick.

The bottom line: Innovation Team formation requires a process that incorporates training in all of these ideas, taking into account the dynamics of group formation. Our experience is that it takes three days and two sleep cycles to do this well. It requires an off-site retreat, where the work of the group in forming themselves as an effective innovation team is the only focus. No distractions from additional agendas or heading home each night. Afterwards it requires constant reinforcement and support following the initial training. That's where the work on establishing a creative environment comes in. We wish it weren't true. We could develop more Innovation Teams if it could be done quicker. But it doesn't happen that way. Sorry. You get what you pay for.

It's tough to do well in less than two sleep cycles!

And believe us, three days is fast. One of the things that enables us to say it can be done that quickly is what we call the "quick win." Like most team development practitioners, we begin with simulations that have no real-world consequences for the group. In other words, we create artificial systems to learn and practice with. As rapidly as possible however, we move into practicing these new and improved Innovation Team behaviors on real world problems that the group is chartered to do something about. To find quick wins.

Nothing builds a team like doing real work together. We work with the team to solve real problems, but we use the work as a way of practicing Innovation Team behaviors and debriefing for the quality of the group's behavior before patting ourselves on the back for the quality of the solution. The focus is on the process, not the work. It's an investment strategy that doesn't seem to make sense at first…focusing on the process, not the work?

It's a strategy that pays. An investment spending strategy which reaps huge dividends. Let us know when your team's going public. We're going to be first in line at the IPO.

Tying Compensation to Team Effectiveness

It's the carrot and the stick. It's the systems approach to supporting the positive behaviors of an innovation team. It's part of creating an environment that supports the work of the team.

When the team does its work well, all of the members benefit. Equally.

When the team does poorly, all of the members suffer. Equally.

Anything else allows hierarchical positioning to slither into the team dynamic. Just like that annoyingly persistent gator.

If there is a reason to form an Innovation Team, there is some problem that needs solving. In the world of work, problems that need solving are all about their effect on the bottom line: the work product of the organization.

So when Innovation Teams do their work, they should begin with a specific, measurable goal in mind and a clear idea of just how the team will benefit at an individual, personal level if that goal is attained. Doing this well requires that some metrics be designed, if they're not already in place, both to measure the current state and track movement to the desired state. And the team must buy in to those metrics.

The actual compensation must be more than job security, a desk plaque, key chain, or nice pat on the back. It must be tangible, real, meaningful and measurable. Money, vacations, training chits, a weekly massage, new suede shoes (make mine blue)…it just has to be truly motivating for the group members. If you want results from a team-based system, it takes a team-based reward system. This is what it takes. Yes, this type of compensation is so against the dominant paradigm that it is admittedly difficult to implement. It is however the essence of what grows American business. Small, entrepreneurial groups of people, sharing the risks and rewards of striving for success. Sounds like a challenge for an Innovation Team.

Punishment via Rewards

Rewards and incentives are an interesting, common, and tricky thing. We so often expect to receive them for things we do right, and we often create them in order to have people do the right things. And they're easy to create.

Clean up your room and you get ice cream

Meet your quota and you get a bonus

Finish by your deadline and get a longer break

Implement a great strategy and you'll get a raise

The problem with rewards and incentives is that as much as they reward behavior, they also create disincentives at the very same time.

For example, we were doing a lot of work creating Innovation Teams with a large consumer goods company. The emphasis was on teamwork, working with others to create new ideas, and implementing strategies. We were trying to change the culture and habits of the organization. Yet we had a lot of trouble getting the change to stick over time. There were several reasons for this, but one of the big ones is that the reward systems still worked on an individual basis.

When annual review came around, the focus was on what the individual accomplished. Never mind the team. Never mind the great ideas that they contributed to other people, or suggestions that others implemented. What did YOU do. Oops. An important incentive/reward program was short-circuiting what the organization really wanted to accomplish.

We know that car dealerships can be scary places to go, because some sales people will do anything to to earn their commission by selling a car. And what is the effect on the customer? They feel pressured, cheated, and screwed over. After all, the sales person's incentive is usually tied only to how many cars they sell. It's not based on how satisfied the customer is. Or whether they come back again (not directly at least). Or whether they were happy with the experience. Or whether they were treated fairly.

What are the hottest growing trends in automobile sales today? The no-dicker-sticker and commission-free sales forces. Saturn has created a very loyal following among customers for their low-pressure sales tactic and selling cars for a flat price by non-commissioned sales people. And consumers love it. Even though they may not love the product (which at this writing is well out-of-date compared to cars they are shopped against), people still go there for easy, pleasant, and pain-free shopping. And finally, other brands and dealerships are taking notice. Jonathan helped his sister buy a new car at a Ford dealership like this recently and it was almost fun (probably because he wasn't writing the check)!

Want to get people to do something? Rewards may be one way of doing it, but be aware of the flip side of the incentive. Look at what the incentive is dis-incenting. Are people relying on the rewards to get them to do what they should be doing anyway? Is the incentive having them sacrifice the long-term interests of the company for their short-term gain? Are the interests of the few overriding the needs of the many?

The golden rule of rewards should be, "Beware the Law of Unintended Consequences." Because that gator will bite you right in the butt when you least expect it. What gets rewarded gets done, but it also means other things don't. And the things that get dropped aren't always the things you want dropped.

For each reward system created, it's important to look at the pluses and the opportunities of the structure (what are the good things that it will create). Also look at the issues that you have about it, specifically, what are the down sides of rewarding a certain behavior? And then see if you can improve the system by using new thinking to overcome those issues.

The reward is a double-edged sword for the Innovation Team, or any other. Be careful about what gets cut.

Creativity is an Attitude

We admit it. We spend a lot of time talking about tools and techniques for creativity and creative thinking. We focus a lot on specific things you can do to foster innovation, when in fact what those techniques are all about is trying to energize an attitude shift. When you get right down to it, creativity and innovation require a shift in perspective. And it's not that one day you shift your attitude and then the next day you are creative. It's not an "on/off" switch. It's more like a dimmer switch (rheostat, for the electrically savvy). It's about dialing up your already bodacious level of creativity. It's about sending more current through wires that have an unlimited capacity. It's about cranking up the voltage and shocking more innovation into the system.

So what are the required attitudes for creativity? The honest-to-Pete, full-bore, internalized, believe-it-or-die attitudes necessary, critical, and essential for high-level, absolutely-breakthrough-creating innovation are as follows:

> 1) In order to have good ideas, you must have lots of ideas.
>
> 2) To make creativity happen you must open your mind to new ideas.
>
> 3) Problems can be solved.
>
> 4) There's more than one right answer.

If you can hear this, get this, internalize this, and embrace this, then a creative attitude is yours. Will it happen just by reading this? No. Can you make it happen by memorizing this? Not nearly enough. Will reciting these attitudes every morning do the trick? Not by itself.

You must practice them, be aware of them, live them, and demonstrate them constantly. Which will take lots and lots of work. Are you ever done? No, of course not. Even Sid Parnes, a pioneer in the study of creativity and the development of creative processes and the best example we know of the creative mind-set in the world, has moments where he slips. Even the Messiah figures in all of the major religious orthodoxies were tempted. So, too, will you be. And you will succumb to the gator brain. Hey, it's okay.

The trick is to get back on top of the (metaphorical) horse that is the creative attitude and to continue the (figurative) long-ride.

Happy (creative) trails.

Attitudes for Creativity:

As simple as the Rubik's cube looks, it's not easy to solve. Similarly, the following attitudes necessary for true innovation look simple. But they're impossible to have in mind all the time. Mastery is an impossible goal. Especially when the Gator is knocking at the door to your brain. But that doesn't mean that you shouldn't try to internalize these as fundamental to your existence...

1) In order to have good ideas, you must have lots of ideas.
2) To make creativity happen, you must open your mind to new ideas.
3) Problems can be solved.
4) There's more than one right answer.

The sooner you get started living these, the more rapidly innovation will take you to success! What are you waiting for?

Recap:

THE MOTTO: In order for us to be successful, (unlike the lottery) everybody has to be the big winner.

Territoriality and the Reptilian Brain - Your gator brain (remember eat, attack or run from newness?) usually takes over whenever there's an opportunity to move up the hierarchy. However, Innovation Team members know that the slickest hierarchy is one that's flexible: sometimes I'm in charge, sometimes you're in charge. But never should the gator brain be running the show, because the gator is looking to protect his/her territory, not the team's.

Growing and Developing Others - Want to win? Want the team to win? Then look for opportunities for other members of the team to win. Share your insights to help them and they will help you. Make them look good and they'll want to make you look good. Growing yourself requires you to grow others. That by itself contributes to your growth, and it makes others want to return the favor. Now isn't that a beautiful symbiotic relationship?

Establishing Group Norms - The best way to get the group working together well is to go away and practice working together. And then spend some time working together on real challenges while all the time being conscious of how the group is working together. Focus on the process, use effective tools and techniques, and actively discuss how to get better. Pay attention to the process, not the work. Paradoxically, it will improve the work!

Tying Compensation to Group Effectiveness - Want the team to work well as a team? Then stop rewarding individuals. Reward the entire team when they succeed, and make the entire team suffer when they do poorly. Even if it was directly attributable to one person. Who's responsibility is the success/failure? The leader. Who's the leader of an Innovation Team? You…and everyone else. Compensate accordingly.

Punishment via Rewards - What is rewarded gets done. What isn't doesn't. The law of unintended consequences takes those two principles and causes big trouble. Evaluate your reward systems carefully to see what the system is and is not rewarding people *to do*, and what it's rewarding people *to not do*. The results may be surprising, and not in a good way.

Creativity is an Attitude - Actually, it's four. Here they are: 1) In order to have good ideas, you must have lots of ideas; 2) To make creativity happen, you must open your mind to new ideas; 3) Problems can be solved; and 4) There's more than one right answer. Now all you have to do is integrate these into your life.

What are some of the places in
your life where you could work to
create win-win relationships?

6

Strive for Constant Improvement

"Anybody can cut prices, but it takes brains to make (something) better."
-- Alice Hubbard

If you've been reading along and didn't just open the book to this page, you've noticed an undercurrent: Grow. Grow. Grow. Then grow some more. Innovation is about expansion, becoming more, creating more. The best way to contribute as fully as possible to an Innovation Team is to bring as much to the table as you possibly can. That means being as much as you possibly can. A dynamic, growing-up makes the best Innovation Team member. Where are your growing edges? What are the current self-improvement strategies you are pursuing? What is your personal mission statement? Any employee of a successful business should be able to answer these questions relative to that business. You should be able to answer these questions relative to the company called YOU.

It's a good idea to break your self-improvement strategies into four interdependent but unique categories as you plan your growth. There are many ways you could divide yourself up in this regard, but for this discussion, we'd suggest you look at four: 1) Your physical self (muscles, bones, organs, immune system etc.), 2) your psychological self (thoughts, emotions, coping mechanisms etc.), 3) your social self (networks, friends, family, place in community etc.) and 4) your spiritual self (connection to that outside of self, sense of meaning, etc.). Short-hand: Bio, Psycho, Social, Spiritual.

In each of these areas, high performance Innovation Team members are working to develop themselves. They are attempting to expand that which they are through increased connection to knowledge, others, the world around them, and their experience of the cosmic mystery. Through this, they are maturing and gaining wisdom. They're doing things as simple as reading a magazine they might not normally pick up, or as complex as spending a month in the wilderness on a quest for their vision. It might be as simple as committing to say, "I love you" to their children more frequently, or as complex as accepting a mentoring relationship with someone.

This is a large part of why Innovation Teams are "the place to be." You get to work with a great group of folks who help you keep growing by setting a standard for constant personal improvement. Grow. Grow. Grow some more.

Brain Hygiene

You brushed your teeth when you got up this morning didn't you? You did your hair, chose your clothes, did something to make sure you don't stink up the elevator at the end of the day...

But have you brushed your brain today?

Come on! Admit the truth. We can see it on your face. What would your mother say?

Sadly, not a darn thing we'd guess. And it's a shame. It just won't do. You see, you could break almost anything on your body and we could either replace it or you could get along fine without it. And of course, we put a lot of energy into making sure our body will keep working for as long as possible. We try to keep our hearts healthy through exercise and diet. We protect our skin with sunscreen. We brush with tartar-removing toothpaste. We get regular physicals at the doctor. But when was the last time you went in for a mental? Probably only if something wasn't working the way it should, but never just to see if there was anything you could do to optimize the function of your brain. What, it's good enough for the hard drive on your computer, but not for your brain?

Since everything to grow and strengthen Innovation Teams requires that the brains of the team members work well, we'll present some things that you could be doing to optimize its function.

Have you brushed your brain today?

First, let us say this. The process of allowing yourself to defer judgment in ideation helps all by itself. The immutable synaptic truth of our brains is "use it or lose it." When your divergent brain is really cooking along you're firing on as many synapses as possible. A good thing.

But even assuming you've got the thinking skills that allow you to utilize as much of the brain as possible -- great brain software if you will -- optimized for your system, there are things that can be done to improve the function of the hardware as well.

You are what you think. You are what you eat. They're both true. If you have choices about what you eat (and if you're far enough up Maslow's Hierarchy of Needs that you have the time to read this, you do) there are some "do's" and "don'ts" that might be wise to follow. A lot has been written about this, and some of it is still controversial, but here are some well agreed upon highlights:

Medical science is able to keep us living for as long as 100 years without much difficulty but in polls of people over 60, most say that they would prefer not to live that long. The single greatest reason: fear of mental decline. You can do something about that. And in so doing, serve the function of your Innovation Team better.

The mind. What a terrible thing to waste.

Idea Time

You'll probably never find it on a clock face, because we're not talking about what time ideas happen (always 4:45). We're talking about the fact that sometimes ideas need time to percolate up through the gray matter into our consciousness.

Remember the four stages of creative generation (as defined by Graham Wallace): 1) Preparation, 2) Incubation, 3) Illumination and 4) Verification.

In a world run by instant gratification, "incubation" becomes harder and harder to have happen. More and more technology makes it difficult to have moments of incubation. We can research, type, spell-check and send a document around the world faster now than it used to take us to get to the library, or get a document back from the steno pool, or edit by hand, or even walk a letter to the post office.

Your brain needs a properly balanced diet to function well.

Eat less fat.

Eat less simple sugar.

Eat fewer simple carbohydrates.

Eat more fruits and vegetables.

Eat more protein from low fat sources.

Eat more unre-fined, complex carbohydrates.

Consider taking mineral supple-ments and multivi-tamins with anti-oxidants.

The system rarely allows us time to think. Deadlines get shorter, demands become greater, and technology conspires against us to reduce turn-around time. So we must force the system. We must take the time to let our brains percolate to create the brilliant ideas that will change the world, rather than settling for the first thing we can come up with.

How do we do that? Do what Einstein did, and take a walk or go sailing. Take Thoreau's advice and go sit by a pond. Follow the lead of Bob and go for a walk in the woods, or follow Jonathan's lead and go swimming…or better yet, sit in a coffeehouse and eat cookies. Bob Lutz went for a drive in the back roads of Michigan (and created the concept for the Dodge Viper). Edison would go fishing…without bait.

Do what it takes to clear your mind and your environment and explore new avenues, both literally and figuratively. It's not easy to do sometimes, especially in the "I need the idea now!" moments. But the rewards, in terms of creative output, will make it all worthwhile.

The Four Stages of Generating an Idea

1) **Preparation**: the time that you take to spend time getting all the information that you need/want/can get about the challenge. It's about understanding the background of that for which you are seeking creative ideas. It's like getting all of the ingredients out to prepare to bake bread and mixing them. Preparation is preparing your mind for…

2) **Incubation**: walking away from the challenge and letting your brain work on the challenge while you're doing other things, like taking a walk, going sailing, working on something else, getting a cup of coffee, taking a shower, watching a movie, or driving your car. Consider this the phase when the bread is in the oven, when you can do something else. While you're focusing on something else, you brain is turning over the challenge in your subconscious and working on the challenge, with the end result being…

3) **Illumination**: this is the moment of "AHA!" or "EUREKA!" or "By jove, I think I've got it," or, "I could have had a V-8!" It's the moment we all think of as the moment of creativity, when everything comes together, the world looks clear, the bread is finally done and the answer is obvious and brilliant, at least until…

4) **Verification**: this is the testing stage. Now we have to make sure that we have the right answer, the one that will really solve the challenge. This is about testing, implementing, or asking others if the idea will actually work. It's tasting the bread to make sure it's delicious and nutritious, so that we're willing to share it with others in the world.

Impacting Your Creative Product

We look at creativity and innovation as having four major (brace yourself for a highly technical word) chunks. These come from Mel Rhodes, a creativity researcher who, in 1961, noted that there were four key elements that make up the definition of creativity:

1) Person
2) Process
3) Environment
4) Product

Okay, more background:

1) Person: this is the part of the creativity equation that takes into account the personal aspects of creativity. It's about things like your creative style, how creative you are, your creative development, and the internal workings of your innovative brain.

2) Process: here's where the tools and techniques come in. Process is about the methods we use to spark our creativity, and the things we do -- both consciously and unconsciously -- to work together or alone to get that innovative brain energized.

3) Environment: both the physical and the psychological environment in which we create. So things like our workspace, the type of chair, the kind of music, the method of lighting, the location and all that makes it up. Also the quality of the climate that surrounds us, regardless of whether or not there is trust in the organization, organizational impediments, resources, or time to create ideas. Consider these the support systems or barriers to innovative brain function.

4) Products: the artifacts of the innovative brain. Whether it's consumer products, poetry, artwork, patents, or pot-holders, (yes we've been knitting) products are the manifestations of our new ideas. They're the artifacts of our creativity. And this is typically the area where most people want to see the benefits of creativity - the results and output.

We are firmly of the opinion that in order to energize an Innovation Team that can generate lots of creative output (product), the team must focus on improving the first three (person, process, and environment). These are the things that are training related, the elements of the equation that can be regularly improved and developed in order to increase the likelihood of regular creative production.

So, want better products? Focus on the people, the processes they use, and the climate that surrounds them. Drive everything towards increased creativity by working on all of the components, instead of just trying to drive the output.

Creating Support Systems

Change doesn't happen without reinforcement. You need two-by-fours to hold up the new roof, at least until that roof becomes a ritualized habit. Said more clearly, when new processes or attitudes are introduced into the organization, the team must create systems, structures, processes or methods to help them happen regularly.

For example, when a group agrees to implement a plan of action, what can they do to make sure that it happens? Some things that we've seen:

Publishing of the plan for the whole organization to see or posting it in a hallway

Having weekly meetings to check on the group's progress

Having a "coach" check in with people regularly to see if the things they promised have actually happened

Celebrating major milestones along the way

Putting schedules as automatic pop-ups in e-mail at deadline time

Weekly lunchtime update meetings

Announcements of successful accomplishments along the way

Friday afternoon meetings to report progress on what they did in the past week and what they'll do next week.

In general they fall into a couple of categories: visual reminders (posted displays/signs/schedules) to keep it top of mind, action-oriented reminders (things that the group can do), and habit-oriented reminders (things that happen on a regular basis).

After the creation of a new habit/idea/plan is completed by

the team, ask (and answer) these questions to guide creation of a support system:

How can we keep this alive during our busy days?

Who can support us in making this happen?

What can we do to ritualize this?

What can we display to remind us to do this?

How can we hold each other accountable?

When will we meet again to check on our progress?

What are the obstacles to us doing this, and what can we do to overcome them?

How can we make this fun?

Without these structures integrated into the Innovation Team repertoire, the new habit/idea/plan has a tendency to be lost in the shuffle of day-to-day work. It becomes like a seedling among the weeds of daily operations, overgrown, crowded out, forgotten, and eventually, killed. What could be more tragic?

How to Treat New Ideas: Praise First (A Reprise)

It's been said that new ideas are like newborns. They need to be nurtured, cared for gently, supported and encouraged. Otherwise they don't last very long.

Yet it's no great surprise to know that the most common reaction to a new idea is to kill it, crush it, or demolish it.

How many documents did you touch today that have been photocopied? Today the photocopier is a business necessity, and it's been a staple of the business world for several decades now. However, in the late 30's, Chester Carlson tried to sell his idea of "xerography" to the big technology companies like IBM and Kodak. They rejected his idea.

But you know how the story ends. After $75 million dollars in research, in 1960 a little known company called Haloid-Xerox (now Xerox) unveiled the first $29,500 Xerox copier with a $95/month lease that included 2,000 free copies (four cents for each additional copy), plus guaranteed maintenance of the temperamental copiers. It was an overnight success 25 years in the making.

A home-run hit that everyone believed in during development? No, not even the development group believed in it. "Various members of our own group would come in and tell me that the damn thing would never work," said John Dessauer, head of the Haloid-Xerox R&D division. Such a limited amount of faith for a product that would eventually become a business staple and turn into a $15 billion business for the company. So what can we learn? Just this: don't kill new ideas before you fairly consider them.

New ideas always look strange!

One way to do that is by using the technique we shared in the chapter, "Understand Responsibility" called "POINt." We mention it again because it has a different meaning in the context of this chapter…and darn it, it's amazingly effective and simple! You'll recall that this technique looks at each idea strategically, affirmatively, and deliberately by assessing the following:

Pluses: What are (at least) three things you like about the idea?

Opportunities: What are (at least) three good things that might result if the idea were implemented?

Issues: What are some concerns/issues you have about the idea (phrased as a question starting with "How to…" or "How might…")

New thinking: What are some ideas you have for how to fix the concerns and overcome the issues you just noted?

Imagine you were in charge of doling out venture capital in the late 30's and some garage-engineer-crackpot named Carlson approached you with his pioneer technology to replace the mimeograph machine. You might use the POINt this way:

Pluses: It's unique. I've never seen anything like it before. And it seems like it would be much cleaner than the mimeograph machine with all that carbon paper and ink. Also, I like that you've proven that the concept does work.

Opportunities: It might be the first product like it on the market, and we'll gain huge market share. And it might lead to a whole new profit center for your company. It might also be possible to expand this worldwide and pay off the development costs even faster.

Issues: How to get your employees to have a stake in the development of this extremely complex technology. And how might you create awareness of your new idea so that people can see how revolutionary it is? Also, it looks like it might be expensive, so how might you price it in a way that businesses can afford one of your copiers? And how can we keep that great smell from the freshly mimeographed papers the teacher hands out?

New thinking: As you know, the first and third concerns were overcome with stock options and leasing respectively. To address the second concern and create awareness of the idea, Xerox used innovative promotional strategies including doing demonstrations of the machine in New York's Grand Central Terminal. And the smell? We wonder how many innovative brain cells *that* stuff killed…

New ideas look strange. They seem impractical. They make us feel uncomfortable, and they change the status quo. But they also unleash fifteen-billion-dollar industries. And the way to make sure that we're part of that success is to avoid prematurely killing ideas and instead judge them fairly and deliberately. With Praise First: that's the POINt.

Seeking Feedback Effectively for Individual and Team Growth

Teams of all varieties that work *effectively* together over the long haul have one thing in common (besides being made up of multiple people): they review their performance on a regular basis to identify what's working and what they can/need to do better. This is also true of people who work effectively.

Seeking feedback can be a bold and dicey thing if the people feeding-back don't do it effectively or productively. As a format, we recommend the POINt technique (see above). In a best case scenario, a team will take five minutes at the end of each meeting to do a quick evaluation, and will spend some time generating ideas to overcome any difficult-to-solve concerns that the group has. (some of the solutions to concerns will be obvious).

The same is true for individuals. Want to find out how to express yourself more effectively or be a better leader? Get some feedback from as many others as possible to see how they view you. Not long ago one of us took the opportunity to ask 14 people for their feedback. "I talked to people like my business partners, my friends, my (now) wife, my parents, my sister, some clients, and administrative staff. I had them run through a Praise First: POINt on me." *Talk about risk-taking!* "But I got great feedback that was useful in raising my self-esteem and self-confidence and I identified some important things that I could work on to improve myself (no, I won't share here...draw your own conclusions...as long as you Praise First). In the process, I discovered that I had a great life already, and there was more that I could do to make it even better."

Bottom line: growth requires input, a strategy, and a target. Only by actively seeking feedback will you find that. Have you taken your risk today? If not, start your interviews right now!

Yet-Thinking

Rob Gilbert, the editor of a great little periodical called, *Bits and Pieces*, sums up people this way, "There are basically two types of people. The people who have the 'I can't do it' attitude and those who have the 'I can't do it YET' attitude." You know people who fit into these categories (also known as "resistors" and "assistors"). And you fit in there, too.

In actual practice, we all fall into both categories depending upon the scenario. So here's the value: practice "yet-thinking." Develop the habit of realizing that even if you *can't* do something now, with some work and development, you can develop the skill, strategy or an alternative method to make it happen.

Ray Kroc didn't become the successful Hamburger-maven as the founder of McDonald's until he was in his fifties. He could have given up on changing the way the world eats, or creating a personal fortune if he'd resigned himself to it. But he saw in himself the potential necessary to create perhaps the most recognizable icon of capitalism, the golden arches.

By taking a good hard look at ourselves and correcting our attitude every time we get negative and defeatist, either alone or in a group, we can cause the mind-shift necessary to create brilliant new ideas, solutions and successes. Train yourself to listen for negative responses, and add a "yet" to it. Are you making a million dollars? Not yet. Is the project a success? Not yet. Are we on schedule to make our deadline? Not yet. Is the team working well together? Not yet. Are there any donuts here? Not *yet*.

By becoming a "yet-thinker" you open the space to create, to be generative, to create something new and better. Try it, practice it, internalize it. And create for yourself the perfect world. But we don't live in a perfect world, you say? Nope, not yet!

The Value of Debriefing

We've developed a habit that has helped us tremendously to increase our quality as trainers and facilitators. At the end of a program, we ask ourselves 1) what went well, 2) what didn't, and 3) how might we strengthen our skills and process before the next event. One of us had a training partner in his younger years at another firm who was glad to give feedback in debriefing, but not interested in receiving any himself. He's no longer a trainer.

It's grow…or die.

Debriefing is one of the most powerful tools we know to leverage the learning of an initiative into the future and stop weakness from growing or becoming habitual. It's not a very radical suggestion when you think about evaluating the *product* that has been created through an initiative and we want you to continue doing that. The radical notion here is that we want you to debrief the process you used. The methods of development. The patterns of interaction. The quality of the group process. The value that various individuals brought to the project. The supportiveness of the environment.

And then work to keep the strengths and overcome any weaknesses you discover as you debrief the *process*, people, and environment. Trust us. Great work will continue to flow and your recent success will move from a "one time thing" to "the way it happens around here."

Debriefing at the level of person, process, and environment rather than just at the level of product (as is the typical habit) is the way you build a great Innovation Team, a great company, and *long term* profitability. Those "flash in the pan" stories we hear about companies that do great because they bring a brilliant product to market, but don't last as firms, are stories of groups of people lazily riding on the coattails of a brilliant product, and not using the opportunity to grow themselves into a lean mean innovation machine.

Someone who did it wrong: People's Express (lost focus)

Someone who did it right: Southwest Airlines (*very* focused and constantly breaking the rules…not the law, the rules).

At the end of each project, or at sensible points along the way with large initiatives, do a "POINt" evaluation for each of these four elements: 1) The people on the team, 2) the processes you used, 3) the environment you were working in, and 4) (finally) the product you created. Find the pluses. Find the opportunities. Surface the issues(and list them in question form). Overcome any key concerns using your best innovation skills to develop new thinking.

Move from grow or die, to live long and prosper. It's only logical.

Pay Attention To All Of The Team Members In The Team Called *You*.

Even if you live on a deserted island all alone, you have help in building your cranial corporation.

At a minimum, you have the subpersonalities that are resident in your psyche. If you had Multiple Personality *Disorder* only one of these personalities would be talking at any given time. Since you probably don't have this disorder, what you've gotten used to is living in a cacophony of internal voices. What you know as your personality is the sum of that chatter. It's useful, when working to improve yourself, to break out these various subpersonalities for examination. Both as a way of developing improvement strategies for them and as a way of more clearly hearing their wisdom.

Yes: talk to yourself! And pay attention. But it's not necessary to do it out loud.

Do you have a part of yourself that inspires you and another one that seems to want to hold you back? I bet you can figure out which one we want you to listen to…

Is there a part of you that seems to be especially good at generating wild and crazy ideas? Unleash it.

Do you have a subpersonality that is patient? Another that is constantly challenging you to be more? One which really enjoys connecting to people in a meaningful way? We bet you do. Energize them.

Do you have a pessimist in residence? A critic who likes to be first to comment? A fearful child who's paralyzed by risk? Send them to summer camp. Use your answering machine to monitor their calls. Make a conscious choice about when you will and won't pick up the phone and let them have their say. You're the boss; they just like to make you forget it from time to time.

Innovation Teams are populated by people who know how to bring the right personalities to the work table at the right time. They do it *by choice*, though not always without a little internal dissent. They're individuals who are conscious that they are driven by choice, not by circumstance. *They* are in control when they want to be. And they choose to be most of the time.

Sometimes, when we're diverging, we give these various subpersonalities the floor for a few moments to see what they might contribute to the discussion. There are lots of names for these personalities and people sometimes try to make this more complicated by getting overly symbolic. Here are some simple perspectives* to view your problem with (costumes optional):

Who are you being right now? What is that person saying about this list? About how it relates to you?

Who would you *like* to be right now? After all, it is your choice!

Recap:

Team Members in the Team Called You:
A critical parent
A warrior
A nurturing parent
A bully
A rebellious child
A coward
A positive, playful child
A magician
A logical person
A manipulator
A king or a queen
A dummy
A tyrant
A lover
A weakling
An addict
A dreamer

THE MOTTO: Nothing, including me, is ever perfect. Everything, including me, can always be better.

Brain Hygiene - To maintain your 1) biological, 2) psychological, 3) sociological and 4) spiritual health, you need a healthy brain. Here's a starting list on how to do that: a) eat a proper diet, b) take appropriate supplements, c) avoid both illegal and legal stimulants and depressants, and d) drink more water.

Idea Time - There is value in doing nothing. It's called "incubation time" and it's a critical part of the process of generating new ideas. It fits into the four stages of creating newness: a) preparation, b) incubation, c) illumination, and d) verification. Since society, culture, and the pace of business continue to limit our time to think, you need to squeeze it into your day. There are lots of ways to fit time in. Got your calendar? One, two, three…schedule!

Impacting your Creative Product - Want 1) more innovative products? Then also pay attention to 2) your processes, 3) your people, and 4) your environment, to make them more supportive of innovation. All of these aspects have direct impact on the creative output. Not to pay attention to all of these dimensions means that the first one (product) isn't as innovative as it could be.

Creating Support Systems - Change doesn't happen without reinforcement, so create systems in your team to make sure that the things you want to have happen actually do take place. Consider: a) displaying important information in public, b) scheduling regular meetings or lunches to advance the cause, c) setting up "coaching" relationships, d) celebrating successes, e) using e-mail to remind people, announcements of accomplishments, or f) holding Friday afternoon check-ins to find out what people did this week and what they'll do next week to advance the mission. If you want change to happen, then do something to make sure it's not forgotten.

How to Treat New Ideas: Praise First - Want a productive system to provide feedback? Try the POINt technique: 1) Praise what's good, 2) look for the positive Opportunities, 3) surface issues as questions that can be solved, and then 4) Develop New Thinking to overcome the concerns you have. It's a simply brilliant way to positively, productively, and fairly give effective feedback.

Seeking Feedback Effectively for Individual and Team Growth - Want the team to get better? Look at what they're doing right and what could be improved. How do you do that? Try the POINt (above). Want to get better yourself? Have people you know look at what you're doing right and what could be improved. How? Praise First: POINt. And be willing to take a risk. The risk of having people evaluate you. Is it worth it? Consider the potentially great payoff: an even better you!

Yet-thinking - You can either be an "I can't do it" person (resistor) or an "I can't do it YET" person (assistor). The attitude shift is subtle, but it makes a huge difference in how you do your work and live your life. We know with whom we'd rather work. How about you? Do you know? Yet?

The Value of Debriefing - All great teams have one key thing in common. They debrief their people, processes, products and environments to find out 1) what went well, 2) what didn't, and 3) how might it be improved? These are the steps that lead to ever-greater levels of performance. Considering the alternative, it's five minutes at the end of your day that can yield big payoffs.

Pay Attention to all of the Team Members in the Team Called You - You are not one person. You're a conglomerate of lots of sub-personalities. They're all designed to help you succeed in given situations. Pay attention to them, and choose carefully who you are in a given situation.

What are some of the areas in which
you would like to improve?

7

Start, Finish,
Start Again

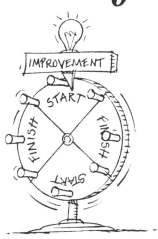

"Don't be afraid to take a big step if one is indicated. You can't cross a chasm in two small jumps."

-- David Lloyd George (1863-1945)
Frmr. British Prime Minister

We've said that it's important to be constantly improving and that you need to have a plan to guide you as you do so. It's also important to create some end points for yourself so that you know when to celebrate. It's critical to honor achievement of goals, both team and personal. It can be a real drag to buy into this "you're never finished" thinking because the amazing potential of human beings offers endless opportunity for improvement. So be absolutely clear what you are heading for (our experience is that people are almost always successful in achieving their vision, so be sure you want it) and when you get there, or make some significant progress, treat yourself or the team to a goodie or two.

Remain constantly vigilant for success-bred arrogance!

But watch out...achieving goals is a dangerous thing too.

We have a tendency to get a little full of ourselves when we reach the goals we've been striving for. Better to take ourselves down a peg before someone else does it for us. So we start again. We remain vigilant for the arrogance that is the "Myth of the Grown-up" (the myth: there are no "grown-ups," only "growing-ups" and stuck people). Sure that it will appear, we watch for it so we can send it away immediately. We surrender to our humanity and take responsibility for the risk of listening so that we can find new opportunities to grow together as a team.

And isn't that why they pay you the big bucks?

Plan for Action

So you need to put together a plan to make things happen? There are lots of ways to do it (some of them even work). What's most important for putting together the plan is that you create one with as much specificity and accountability as possible. There are lots of plans that end up on shelves collecting dust (usually labeled, "strategic plans," sometimes called, "New Year's resolutions"). However, if your team really wants to accomplish something, you'll need to create one to which you're totally committed.

A good plan for action is made up of the following elements:

What is going to be done:

This is the action step, the activity, the tactic, and the thing that will actually take place. It is not a broad strategy or a statement of a theme or category. It is not something like "communicate." It is as specific as possible and includes as much detail as possible, and always a verb, such as, "hold weekly meetings in the staff room to update the team on the progress of Initiative X." Put in as much detail as you possibly can, even if you run the risk of insulting someone by stating the obvious.

Who is going to do it:

Okay, this one's pretty straightforward. Who will take on the responsibility for doing the what? And before this turns into an Abbott and Costello routine, let's just mention this little tidbit: before you put someone on the action plan, make sure they know they're accountable for it! It's so easy to assign Biff to make it happen, especially if he's not in the room. So it's best to avoid that, or to add an action step that tells someone in the room to let Biff know that he has some tasks to do.

By when will it be done:

What's the deadline for accomplishing it? Give a specific date, and better yet, also a time. "In three weeks" means something now, but in three weeks it still means "three weeks later." And that means it may never get done. Oops. What time of what day of what month of what year will it be done?

Who needs to know, or who will support:

Here's the teamwork part. If someone needs to be advised of the completion of a step so that they can move forward on their next step, make sure that is explicit. Also, if there's someone who can assist in making the action step happen, add that too. For the team that's really into accountability, you can add this as a "who will check to confirm?" Or rather, who will be the "designated loving nag?" Nothing gets a project done like the knowledge that someone will follow-up to make sure it's done, and will continue to check on (nag) you until it is!

The pain/pleasure map:

Everything human beings do moves toward pleasure or away from pain. Everything. If there is something that's not getting done, either in your personal life or on your Innovation Team, it's because the "getting it done" is seen as producing more pain than pleasure. Likewise, "keeping the status quo" is seen as producing more pleasure than pain. As illogical as this perspective is sometimes, it is the root of resistance to change and improvement. So here's what you do. Create an absolutely clear vision and a well-explained plan for pain if there is no improvement. Be clear with yourself what happens if you do nothing. Then create a clear vision and plan for the pleasure if there is improvement. Make explicit how wonderful it will be when you make the change. Write both down, draw them, discuss them, do whatever you can to make it as real and tangible as possible. By explicitly stating where the pain and pleasure really lie, you'll rewire your consciousness. This creates the motivation you need to cause the change. Rewire the team's pain and pleasure perspective and you'll produce. Guaranteed!

Reverse the pain and pleasure wiring

The most important thing is to add in as much detail and accountability as possible. This is a discipline that will make or break an Innovation Team. And like most things, the magic isn't in the technique, but the commitment to making it happen and being deliberate about keeping it alive. Regularly.

Planning for action is easy. It's making that action happen that's difficult. But without it, there is no success.

Celebration

As your Innovation Team moves forward and accomplishes the "stuff" it has set as its mission, it's important to take the time to enjoy the energy of accomplishment. We need breaks. We need points in our lives where we honor what we as a team have accomplished. We need a party every once in a while. If you've been doing the work that we've outlined in this book, there is something to celebrate besides just the work product delivered. Celebrate the way you've done your work! Not only have you been doing what you get paid the big bucks to do, but you've been developing yourself as a human being as well. Ultimately, in the big scheme of things, working to improve yourself is the more important of the two. And, truth be told, developing yourself has huge positive implications for your ability to strengthen the bottom line. Congratulations! You're making a difference, and you're doing it in style.

Way to go!

Recap:

THE MOTTO: I'm never perfect. When I remain vigilant for my arrogance, I find my next opportunity for improvement.

Just when you thought you were done - Rats. Curses. Foiled again. Cakes are done. Work is done. Dinner is done. We are never done! Just when we think we've got it all figured out, we discover our arrogance getting in the way of doing it well, since nobody's going to tell us anything. Do you think you know everything? If the answer is yes, then clearly you have more to learn! Remember, there are only growing-up people and stuck people.

Plan for Action - If you want to get to a place where a project is complete, then you'll need a plan of action that incorporates 1) what is going to be done, 2) by whom, 3) by when, 4) detailing who needs to know it's done or who will support it. And don't forget 5) the map detailing the rewards of finishing and the pain that will be caused by not completing the plan. Just remember that the more detail and accountability there is in the plan, the more likely you are to achieve the action you want!

Celebration - Recognizing the end of a project with a party isn't just a lot of fun, it's also critical to motivating the team and recognizing successful contributions. So celebrate the completed project and celebrate the way that you've done your work. Being a member of an Innovation Team isn't easy, so it's something to be rewarded. Because it means you're working with others in an extraordinary way to accomplish amazing things. What better excuse can you think of for throwing a party?

What are the areas in which you need to be ever-vigilant for your arrogance?

Conclusion

"The journey is the reward."

-- Chinese Saying

Once again, the seven key areas to pay attention to as you work to function as an innovative person on an Innovation Team that accomplishes amazingly innovative results in a healthy and productive way are:

> Surrender to humanity
>
> Understand responsibility
>
> Conscious Listening, Clear Speaking
>
> Cultivate Risk Taking
>
> Expect Win-Win
>
> Strive for Constant Improvement
>
> Start, Finish, Start Again

We state unequivocally that this is only one way to articulate the path to success. Lots of people have explored and explained the path; we're just adding a spin to it that hopefully makes it more relevant to our time and our culture. And hopefully, a touch more wisdom as we grow as the species we call humanity.

Envision this growth process as movement up a spiral. The big Slinky® of our life's evolution. We keep learning these same lessons over and over, but each time, at a higher order of understanding. We keep relearning the skills of personal improvement, at each round on the spiral, a higher level of mastery. Yes, the same gosh-darned lessons again and again. Hopefully though, with a more enlightened perspective each time.

Imagine this to be the double helix of an evolved team. The DNA of innovation. The genetic coding for great groups. On one side of the helix are the values we've articulated, the other side are the innovation skills. The ladder rungs of the helix that hold it together are the success strategies. If we're going to solve the bigger more pernicious problems that plague the world, we're going to have to climb that ladder together. We're going to have to evolve in the quality of our relationships and the skill with which we solve problems. We are, in fact, going to have to create one very large Global Innovation Team (G.I.T.). One that is bigger than our work group, bigger than our company, bigger than our community and which crosses our national boundaries. A big, audacious, unprecedented G.I.T.

So buckle up and GIT goin' pardner, we need you on the team!

And good luck on your journey. Just remember. When you think you've arrived, start again.

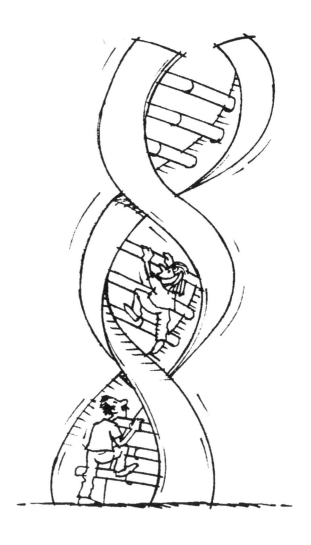

For More Information

If you like what you've read here, following is a list of other books you might find valuable as well, since growth is never complete:

Cameron, J., with Brian, M. (1992). *The Artist's Way: A Spiritual Path to Higher Creativity*. New York: Putnam

Firestien, R. L. (1996). *Leading on the Creative Edge*. Colorado Springs, CO: Pinon Press.

Firestien, R. L. (1998). *Why Didn't I Think of That? A Personal and Professional Guide to Better Ideas and Decision Making*. Buffalo, NY: Innovation Systems Group.

Frankl, Viktor E. (1984). *Man's Search for Meaning* (3rd Revised Edition). New York: Simon & Schuster.

Hall, D. (1997). *The Maverick Mindset: Finding the courage to Journey from Fear to Freedom*. New York: Simon & Schuster.

Hirshberg, J. (1998). *The Creative Priority: Driving Innovative Business In the Real World*. New York: HarperBusiness.

Kohn, A. (1993). *Punished by Rewards: The Trouble with Gold Stars, Incentive Plans, A's, Praise, and Other Bribes*. Boston: Houghton Mifflin.

Lundin, S. C.; Paul, Harry; and Christensen, John (2000). *Fish: A Remarkable Way to Boost Morale and Improve Results*. Hyperion: New York.

MacKenzie, G. (1996). *Orbiting the Giant Hairball: A Corporate Fool's Guide to Surviving with Grace*. New York: Viking.

Moore, R. and Gillette, D. (1990). *King, Warrior, Magician, Lover: Rediscovering the Archetypes of the Mature Masculine*. San Francisco: Harper.

Osborn, A. F. (1993). *Applied Imagination* (3rd Revised Edition). Buffalo, NY: Creative Education Foundation.

Parnes, S. J. (1997). *Optimize the Magic of Your Mind*. Buffalo, NY: Bearly Limited and the Creative Education Foundation.

Peck, M. S. (1978). *The Road Less Traveled: A New Psychology of Love, Traditional Values, and Spiritual Growth*. New York: Touchstone.

Peters, T. (1997). *The Circle of Innovation: You Can't Shrink Your Way to Greatness*. New York: Vintage.

Trout, J. (1999). *The Power of Simplicity: A Management Guide to Cutting Through the Nonsense and Doing Things Right*. New York: McGraw-Hill.

Sure, we've missed some. Please tell us what we missed or what else we should be reading to help us grow. E-mail us at: info@newandimproved.com

Please Help Us Improve!

Thanks for reading our book! We're proud of the work we've put into it, but we know that it's not complete yet (probably never will be…sigh). That said, we're looking for some input from you:

1) Rave Reviews: to help us tell others what's good about it (either in promotional literature, the back cover, our web site, etc.). Please let us know if we can include your name, title, and organizational affiliation (e.g. where you work).

2) Suggestions for improvement: to help us make it more effective, stronger, better, more powerful, or faster than a speeding bullet. If you can phrase it as a question for us to solve, that'd be great! For example, "it stunk" isn't really a helpful suggestion, even if you believe it to be true. However, input such as, "How might you make it more interactive" is actually quite useful.

Please send your input to us at:

E-MAIL:

> info@newandimproved.com

SNAIL MAIL:

> New & Improved
> 9306 State Route 30
> Paul Smiths, NY 12970

Thank you!

Shameless Self-Promotion of our Company

New & Improved teaches people how to summon creativity on demand to solve problems and produce unprecedented results, both professionally and personally. Our organizational development work focuses on developing people skills for innovation ("Innovation Teams" and "Innovation Leadership") and takes various forms including:

Training programs

Keynote speeches

Meeting Facilitation

Individual Coaching

Often, we amalgamate these forms and design an integrated hybrid. No matter what form it takes, we use a proven process and the tools, techniques, and temperament-shifts necessary to infuse innovation into your organization and sustain a creative environment over time. And, we deliver it with energy in a way that's interactive and fun.

What's different about us is that we don't tell you what to do. We teach or facilitate you through a process to leverage the creative potential and knowledge of your people. After all, no one knows your business like you do. So the combination is unbeatable. With your expertise and our proven innovation process, we'll create new ways of achieving success for your organization.

Bottom line: "Innovative Brains" that generate New & Improved anything -- from solutions, strategies and systems, to processes, products and people. Reach us at:

info@newandimproved.com
518-327-3554 east coast USA phone
847-570-0725 mid-west USA phone

About the Authors:

Jonathan Vehar and Robert "Bob" Eckert are Senior Partners at New & Improved, a consulting company that works with a range of organizations to create Innovation Teams: teams who work together productively to create innovation. Their quick wit, piercing insights and commitment to excellence create powerful programs in the areas of creative thinking, team development, strategic planning, creative problem solving, leadership development and meeting facilitation.

Some of the organizations to benefit from their training and facilitation include: Disney; Clorox; Deloitte & Touche; GE; General Mills; Kodak; Kraft; Merck; Nestle; New York State Department of State; Nokia; Pfizer; Xerox; and the US Navy, as well as many social service agencies and school systems.

Jonathan was formerly the Director of Training and Consulting for the Creative Education Foundation and prior to that worked in the field of advertising and marketing. He holds a Master's Degree in Innovation and Change Leadership from the State University of New York. They are both regular instructors at the Creative Problem Solving Institute.

Bob speaks from a background which includes: management experience in both manufacturing and retail, work as a family therapist, creation/direction of the nationally renowned Leadership and Healthy Lifestyles program, teaching in both youth and adult criminal justice systems, and work as a senior "Outward Bound" instructor for incarcerated juveniles. He is on the design team for the Creative Education Foundation's Global Odyssey program.

Bob lives with his family, works and tends his tree farm in the northern Adirondack Mountains near Lake Placid, NY.

Jonathan and his wife live in Evanston, IL, and when he's not working, he can be found racing sailboats, swimming, and unsuccessfully trying to avoid Chicago winters.

Index